DUNGEONS & DRAGONS®

Heroes' Feast
FLAVORS OF THE MULTIVERSE
AN OFFICIAL D&D COOKBOOK

KYLE NEWMAN · JON PETERSON · MICHAEL WITWER · SAM WITWER

RECIPES BY ADAM RIED

PHOTOGRAPHS BY RAY KACHATORIAN

TEN SPEED PRESS
California | New York

CONTENTS

INTRODUCTION

Can you name a tabletop activity that is highly social, builds community, and has infinite possibilities? If you said dining with friends, you're right. If you said Dungeons & Dragons, you're also right! Today, some fifty million people have played the game; D&D-inspired shows and movies top the charts; licensed D&D products fill retail shelves (ahem); and video games based on D&D's concepts rule the screens. In short, D&D is everywhere—including the kitchen!

Initially published in 1974, Dungeons & Dragons was the world's first role-playing game and would go on to revolutionize all aspects of the gaming industry and pop culture alongside it. It introduced an array of now-pervasive gaming concepts, from leveling up to gamified role assumption, but it notably held on to some aspects of its war-gaming past. Born out of a gaming culture that prized realistic simulation, the notion of needing food was inherent in the earliest versions of the game, usually represented in the simple tracking of weekly rations. To have any hope of surviving a protracted excursion in the dungeon underworld, you needed to stay fed. Simply put, in D&D, you must eat to live. But adventurers also needed a place to meet, carouse, and gather information, and what better venues to place in front of them than taverns, public houses, and other places of food and drink?

As the game developed through different communities, food became a key part of the game's narrative experience. In many of the early modules, it was not uncommon for taverns to have long lists of food and drink from which adventurers could choose. For example, in the iconic *Keep on the Borderlands*, adventurers have the option of no less than five drinks and eight dishes, from honey mead and bark tea to pudding and roast joint. By the time the *Forgotten Realms* campaign world was in full force, there were entire books devoted to rating and discussing inns and dining establishments (thanks, Volo!). More cosmopolitan venues in the multiverse boasted restaurants that might seem worthy of a Michelin star or two.

Why so many options for an element of realism that could just as simply check the box? Perhaps it's because early designers realized that food could provide new avenues for the narrative experience. Would a haughty aristocrat be content with iron rations? How well can that halfling hold her drink and what does she do when she doesn't? This is to say, the unexpected, memorable, and hilarious moments of any given D&D session are as likely to come up over an in-game tankard of Neverwinter Nectar (page 30) as they are while battling a feisty gaggle of kobolds.

In the first book, *Heroes' Feast: The Official D&D Cookbook*, we posed the question, "How can food elevate and enhance the D&D experience?" In *Heroes' Feast Flavors of the Multiverse*, we ask, "How can cooking and dining play an essential part of the communal gaming experience?" The book that you are holding is both a guide to D&D food and a culinary companion to your game nights. It includes more than seventy-five delicious recipes, which you can enjoy alongside your in-game character. We've even created some food-loving characters of our own (once nameless adventurers taken straight from the cover of the first *Heroes' Feast*) whose madcap, multiversal adventures provide the locational basis for the dishes herein. Our hope is that this book not only adds a visceral and delicious element to your games but also becomes another avenue to connect with fellow gamers. So, in the immortal words of the original *Player's Handbook*, "enjoy, and may the dice be good to you."

ABOUT THIS BOOK: COOKING FANTASIES

Dungeons & Dragons is a game based on imagination, and so is this cookbook. But, of course, everything is spawned by something else, and the worlds of D&D are no different. From bustling port-side cities to sprawling pastoral landscapes, the game is full of real-world influences, and this is also true of what adventurers may eat. Whether your character frequents the taverns of the Forgotten Realms, the castles of Greyhawk, or the forests of Krynn, there's a good chance you'll see something familiar on the menu. That's because roast meats, hearty grains, and seasoned vegetables are as ubiquitous in the D&D multiverse as they are in our world. The main differences come in the specific ingredients that are used and the way they are prepared.

One challenge that arises when trying to bring any aspect of D&D to life is feasibility. You may wonder, "Do I need spells, magical items, and mystical ingredients to make this stuff?" Rest assured, the answer is "no." The chef and author team have spent countless hours ensuring that each dish is true to its D&D world but also possible to prepare with ingredients and techniques available in ours. We've even consulted the great archmage Mordenkainen, who has assured us that our substitutions and alternate techniques "usually improve the dish" (he's a curmudgeon and that's high praise from the Lord Mage of Greyhawk). When the original recipe calls for rothé, we'll give you a reasonable analog, such as prime beef. Owlbear milk can be a bit hard to find in these parts, but not buttermilk, which offers a similar tang and texture. While the herring from the Rock of Bral may boast a unique flavor, North Atlantic smoked kipper is a suitable substitute. Ultimately, our approach to creating this collection of recipes was to collect and curate the most notable dishes in the D&D multiverse; adapt them for feasibility and flavor; and present them in a manner that even a first level chef

might be able to prepare successfully. Accordingly, our master chef has not only conjured easy-to-follow recipes but also some helpful Cook's Notes, which will guide you through every aspect of the journey.

"Adventuring Gear"

Like a lich's lair, the road of culinary adventure has the potential for disaster and reward. Only with a fair amount of skill, perseverance, caution, and luck do you have a chance of survival. But before you embark on this journey, you'll also need the right gear. While fighters wield their swords and shields, and mages have their staffs and spellbooks, those who practice the culinary arts also require the proper implements to ensure a successful quest. Here are some tools that will help you complete this adventure and perhaps even level up along the way:

- **Baking sheets**
- **Bench scraper**
- **Blender**
- **Cheese grater**
- **Chef's knife**
- **Cocktail shaker and muddler**
- **Colander**
- **Dutch oven or sauté pan**
- **Food processor**
- **Garlic press**
- **Loaf pan**
- **Measuring cups and spoons**
- **Mixing bowls**

- **Muffin tin**
- **Nonstick and cast-iron skillets**
- **Parchment paper**
- **Pastry brush**
- **Pie plate**
- **Saucepans**
- **Spatulas**
- **Stand mixer or electric handheld mixer**
- **Standard cooking utensils, such as cooking spoons, tongs, whisk**
- **Strainer**
- **Vegetable peeler**
- **Wire racks**

The Inn of the Last Home
Main Road, Last Home (North) Solace

food

. . . . 4 stl	Rabbit, mustard-rubbed and long rice	5 stl
e & nuts . . . 3 stl	Pheasant with breads and wine gravy	6 stl
. . . . 1 stl	Shrimp (Tarsis style)	7 stl
. . . . 2 stl	Twice-fried sausages & twice-baked potatoes	5 stl
. . . . 1 stl	Tika's Stewed Woodchuck with seasonal roots	5 stl
. . . . 3 stl	Quince cheese hand pie	1 stl
. . . . 2 stl	Honeyed fig tarts	2 stl
. . . . 3 stl	Sour cream Walnut Cake by the slice	2 stl
. . . . 3 stl	Dortberry pie by the slice	2 stl
. . . . 3 stl	Sliced fruits and fresh cream	1 stl
h cream . . . 1 stl	Kender kiffles	1 stl
and onion . . . 3 stl	Quith pa table nosh	On the house
. . . . 4 stl		(as long as you're drinking)

drinks

WORLDS OF FLAVOR

Dungeons & Dragons comprises numerous campaign settings, and each is traditionally based on a single planet or realm rich with its own histories, mythologies, cultures, and, of course, culinary identities. Several locales from this vast multiverse are explored within this cookbook, forming the basis on which the recipes are organized. While each location is built for in-game action and intrigue, they also yield their own ingredients, traditions, and techniques that promise culinary adventure. These include:

Forgotten Realms

The Forgotten Realms is an epic fantasy setting bursting with memorable characters, distinctive locales, and a deeply layered mythology. Created by Ed Greenwood, the Earthlike planet called Toril is home to this sprawling and diverse campaign world spread across several key continents, the most famous of which is Faerûn (beneath which the Underdark lurks). Each offers vast and eclectic topographies, dense with medieval-style cities and ports. Faerûn boasts some of the game's most storied regions, including the Sword Coast, Amn, Calimshan, Cormyr, the Dalelands, Icewind Dale, and Thay, as well as the legendary cities of Baldur's Gate, Calimport, Neverwinter, Waterdeep, and the infamous Underdark metropolis of Menzoberranzan. The cuisine of Toril is as varied as the settings themselves, from dishes inspired by medieval Europe to tastes derived from Asia as well as the Americas.

Dragonlance

Developed by Tracy Hickman and Margaret Weis, Dragonlance depicts a dreamy, high-fantasy world of purple mountains; forested, evergreen trails; crystal lakes; and dragons of every color. Despite its natural beauty, Dragonlance's planet of Krynn is a world ravaged by war. Here, magic is rare and humanoids constantly find themselves at the mercy of dragons and dragonkind. Some seek harmony and cosmic balance, others crave control and domination. Ansalon is the most well-known of the planet's five continents, and it includes many of the famous locations from the campaign's bestselling novels, including Istar, Kalaman, Pax Tharkas, Qualinost, Qué-Shu, Silvanost, Solace, Solamnia, Tarsis, and Xak Tsaroth. The food of this lush world ranges from European tavern fare to vibrant flavors found throughout Asia.

Spelljammer

Its design originally helmed by Jeff Grubb, Spelljammer is a wholly unique setting that launched Dungeons & Dragons into the stars and cleverly allowed travel between the traditionally isolated sword-and-sorcery worlds of D&D. On board magical flying ships called spelljammers, players can traverse the Astral Plane, a vast expanse of interplanetary space, to celestial destinations untold. It not only provided canonical means for characters (and their stories) to migrate between planets but it birthed an endless ocean of new adventures, adversaries, and locations to explore—and with it, endless swashbuckling hijinks. Storied locales such as the Rock of Bral, an intergalactic spaceport orbiting the planet Toril, conjure a healthy dose of space fantasy tropes. With a cosmic "open sea" vaster than any planetary ocean, an explosion of cultures and cuisines are invariably on offer to enliven any campaign.

Greyhawk

The homebrew campaign setting of D&D co-creator Gary Gygax, Greyhawk is a grounded, sword-and-sorcery-style world rife with forbidden magic and perilous dungeons. This campaign is set on a sprawling, ocean-laden planet called Oerth, with medieval sensibilities and overt shades of Earth. Several continents cluster the surface of Oerth, including Hepmonaland, Hyperboria, and, most notably Oerik, which hosts an area called the Flanaess on its eastern part. The Flanaess is home to Greyhawk's most documented regions and kingdoms, including Perrenland, the Shield Lands, Urnst, Iuz, Veluna, Keoland, Sunndi, and Furyondy. Fabled cities and dungeons mark these areas from the Free City of Greyhawk, the Village of Hommlet, and White Plume Mountain to Saltmarsh, Blackmoor, and beyond. Greyhawk's cuisine culls its inspiration from feudal Europe, especially Britain, often with a fantastical twist.

Eberron

Eberron is a steampunk-styled world of swashbuckling adventure, where incredible machines and potent magic improbably coexist. Invented by Keith Baker, the planet consists of several continents, the most famous of which is Khorvaire. There, the eclectic Five Nations of Aundair, Breland, the Mournland (Cyre), Karrnath, and Thrane contend for supremacy over the ruined Kingdom of Galifar. From the shimmering towers of Sharn to the ruin-filled port city of Stormreach, this visionary, war-torn campaign boasts vibrant cuisine uniquely representative of the Five Nations. Eberron's tastes range from unpretentious feudal fare to exquisitely sophisticated epicurean creations made with a delightful blend of magic and many-geared machines.

Planescape

Designed by David "Zeb" Cook, the campaign setting known as Planescape fittingly takes place in the Outlands, which in the cosmology of the Outer Planes is the center of the Great Wheel. According to Jeff Grubb's 1987 *Manual of the Planes,* a mysterious shaft known as the Spire rests at the center of the Outlands; seven years later the Planescape campaign set atop it the famed city of Sigil. This City of Doors, as Sigil is affectionately known to multiplanar travelers, serves as a conduit to the myriad worlds that comprise the

D&D multiverse. Considered to be "the center of the universe," Sigil is a multicultural nexus, which unifies these seemingly infinite, interdimensional magical portals to dimensions untold. Though numerous planes are connected to Sigil—such as the Astral and Prime Material Planes—Sigil cannot be accessed by conventional travel and can be entered only via one of the many gateways that lead to the different worlds and planes. A city unlike any other, Sigil is crowded with structures stacked and layered upon themselves, while new buildings, courtyards, and streets are constantly being constructed, perpetually altering the city's already eclectic landscape. It should come as no surprise that the cultures and flavors on offer are constantly evolving, ensuring that no two visits or meals in Sigil will ever be the same.

PLANE FOOD

The D&D multiverse is made up not only of myriad worlds but of other dimensions or "planes of existence." The standard "reality" that most experience in these realms is called the Prime Material Plane, but this dimension is just the tip of the iceberg. It is believed that these worlds are surrounded by planes, some of which are "echo" realities that exist in the same cosmological space as the Material Plane, while others are spatially and conceptually much farther afield, such as the planes of the gods. Like the worlds they surround, each of these planar locales, from the Nine Hells of Baator to Seven Heavens of Celestia, has its own character, and even cuisine, including the Feywild and the Shadowfell.

The Feywild

Sometimes called the Plane of Faerie, the Feywild is a dreamy, haunting reflection of the Material Plane, known for its indescribable beauty. Bathed in eternal dawn, its verdant and alluring woodland landscapes are the native home to the fey and harengon, creatures of unparalleled wonder. The Feywild, much like its Shadowfell counterpart, is an echo of the Material Plane. But unlike the Shadowfell, it is a tantalizingly

positive and vibrant place of joy, where each of its parallel locations is grander and more majestic. It is a rare locus of unrefined magic, unrestrained emotion, and unbridled passion, an ancient land birthed of love, laughter, and mischief. In the Feywild, scents are stronger, colors more vivid, sounds clearer, and flavors more remarkable, making any culinary experience that much more memorable.

The Shadowfell

The Shadowfell, commonly referred to as the Plane of Shadow, is a dark reflection of the Prime Material Plane. Unlike its "echo" opposite, the Feywild, the Shadowfell is a bleak, desolate region draped in an eternal twilight, veiled in gloom, and synonymous with death. Since its primary inhabitants are cursed creatures of the night, as well as the dead, the Shadowfell is largely void of life and hope. In its darkest corners, where sinister powers fester, the Domains of Dread lie in wait. These haze-shrouded demiplanes are places of unimaginable horror ruled by sadistic lords who consider these private domains their own perverse paradise. Many of the individual domains that make up the demiplanes were originally dragged from the Prime Material Plane and tethered to the Shadowfell by powerful magical mists. The same impenetrable mists that border these doomed areas prohibit travel to other planes through any conventional means. In the Shadowfell, and its Domains of Dread, one's primary senses are gradually muted, resulting in an insipid culinary experience regardless of what is consumed.

Ravenloft

Originally published in 1983 as an *Advanced Dungeons & Dragons* module by designers Tracy and Laura Hickman, Ravenloft is both a campaign setting and the legendary castle of vampire Strahd von Zarovich, located in D&D's most famous Domain of Dread: Barovia. Accessible by way of the Shadowfell (and usually by mistake), this sprawling Gothic Horror landscape, which remains eternally shrouded in mist, has served up generations of nightmares courtesy of Strahd, his throngs of undead minions, and his dark hold on the demiplane.

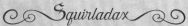

Squirladax

Huzzah and welcome to the journal of the Bureau of Dark Tables, adventurers and gastro-gnomes extraordinaire! I, Squirladax the Goblin Poet, leader of the Bureau, pledge to you that the thrills herein are purely factual and scribed roughly as they occur! For this record is penned with an item of mighty power: the Quill of Scrivening! How works this? One need only speak words into its flaxen feather and watch as a ghostly hand scribes them into one's adventurer's journal! Miraculous!

As such, even I, wise as I am, know not what will fill these pages! As I stand on the precipice of undreamed-of adventure, my heart is full. Yet, in truth, my guts are stewed with the juices of uncertainty and the spices of regret.

What means this? Kind reader, I do not intend to spoil your sweet puddings with my sour tumults, but the Bureau was very recently upended. One cannot feast of the sweet meats and cheeses of life without paying the bill, eventually. Hath you ever heard of the dread utterings referred to only in hushed tones as a TPK? I can feel your trembling hands grasp a term your mind refuses to ingest. Yes, my party hath just suffered a **T**otal **P**lanning **K**atastrophe.

Now, before you leap to conclusions, I wish it known that 'twasn't **my planning** that caused the cleavèd limbs and screaming death of my comrades. As leader, I am but a humble chef of sorts, and I can only make as fine a meal as my ingredients permit. My ingredients were perhaps a bit too fresh, and **their** lack of ripeness was their undoing.

Eight young adventurers stood forth, many lacking in grit, and all too young to appreciate my inspirational bardic magic. Their cowardice flowed like wine. And there was not a single cleric-healer among us, and that much 'twas on me! For it is well understood in all adventuring literature, from guild manuals to the guides of Volo, that a proper party must haveth might for the front lines, magic to rain down destruction from afar, healing hands to restore vigor, and of course a great mastermind to control—nay—**lead** them all.

Any of ways, that chapter is closed. But, let it be said—TWO of their number survived and so too did a portion of our treasure! A fine—if slightly chippèd—RUBY, which I have named, well, Ruby. As they have survived, I have survived, and Ruby has survived, so too does the Bureau of Dark Tables survive!

Failure is the fire by which we cook tomorrow's victories, and I am burning with excitement for what 'tis next. I promise thee, fearless reader, that I shall have my victory. A QUEST will present itself. The Tables will be turned, and one day I shall return to my beloved homeland—the Caves of Calmness—with riches untold.

Onward and Bree-Yark!

The Bureau of Dark Gables

Squirladax
POET AND BARD OF MAGLUBIYET

Sasha
FIGHTER AND FITNESS ENTHUSIAST

Deelia
SORCERESS AND SERVANT OF THE RAVEN QUEEN

Bri'An
EXALTED CLERIC OF TYR

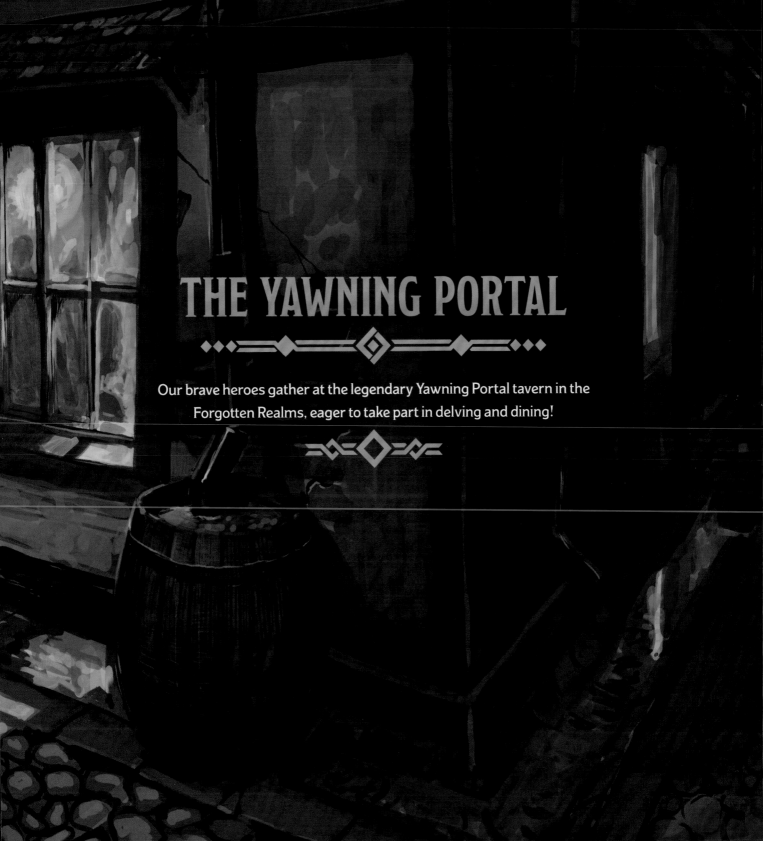

THE YAWNING PORTAL

Our brave heroes gather at the legendary Yawning Portal tavern in the
Forgotten Realms, eager to take part in delving and dining!

Deelia

The Yawning Portal. Cursed reader, if you are unfamiliar with this place, let me be the first to admonish and congratulate you. If you have never been, **do not go**. If you have gone, do not come back. . . .

It is a tavern. A place of merriment for all. It is also a cork—a giant stopper on a jug of poisoned wine, for the Yawning Portal is built on top of a giant stone well that plummets fathoms down into the tunnels of the mad mage Halaster. They call it Undermountain, and it is down there that the soulless corpses of failed adventurers feed carrion crawlers and worse.

But up here, all is laughter, and the amber light of candles and sconces glow amid wafting aromas of faraway spices. Up here, the bodies have animated, haughty, mirthful expressions. Up here the bodies still have souls.

That's where I come in.

I am Deelia, collector of souls. Why am I here? Because Squirladax has proclaimed that we "do our part" in this year's "Great Delving." Apparently, the idea is that one drinks and feasts at the tables poised about the gaping well that falls to the dungeons below. When an adventurer's group has its glut of rothé steak or sornstag, that group boards a sturdy "elevator" platform, dangling from ropes above this pit. It is then that the pulleys squeal, and the group makes its slow descent to Undermountain to "battle evil." It's a party.

Group after group go down, and groups minus one or more come back up, often with grievous wounds rebuking the mirth of hours before. It is for this reason that the Yawning Portal's swarthy proprietor Durnan hires clerics and those of magical salves to await the broken adventurers to heal their wounds and hopefully save lives.

So, of course, Squirladax—wielding one stone to murder many birds—has invited a pious little dragonborn cleric named By'ron (or something) to join our Bureau. He shall mend holes in our holey purses, for every life he saves here brings to us needed coin.

And if the lives cannot be saved, well, I am here to whisper a word of guidance to their souls to send them . . . elsewhere.

Sasha

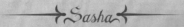

So, we're super short on money—I hope no one minds that I ordered the cow butter. I do believe this is a business expense. According to my new/used *Volo's Guide to Bodily Health*, gifted to me by wise Squirladax, "a washing of wounds in rich butters" will totally "oil the joints" and give me the speed and agility that I lacked in the . . . uh . . . TPK. Oh crap! I ordered the SALTED butter! Oh well . . . As *Volo's Guide* says, "There is no gain without pain." Maybe I should order some of those "famous" Yawning Portal biscuits to lather the excess on. I'm freaking starving!

Deelia

Ugh. Bri'An (I guess is his name) has laid many benedictions at the lip of the chasmal well to various so-called adventurers. "Tyr be with the brave." "Tyr guide and protect you."

Tyr can suckle the worms from their guts.

So far, three groups have descended to Undermountain. None have returned of yet. My tankard of Neverwinter Nectar is running low. As is my patience.

I spy pathetic Squirladax cradling that sad bit of ruby he treasures.

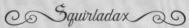

Squirladax

BISCUITS?! NECTARS?! These I did not authorize! There shall NOT be foods to cram into our filthy mouth-holes, I commanded, for I do not trust THESE PRICES! We have a plan and must stick't'it! Soon, wounded heroes will appear up from the well, Bri'An will mutter holy jumblings of healing miracles, we will collect coin, then off we will abscond with heavy purses! Any are welcome to persuade me otherwise, but the charisma of my minions sags lowly. I chortle at their famishment!

Deelia

The nectar and Butternut Beer have buoyed me to a bouncy slosh. Eleven groups have descended and FINALLY, Undermountain spews these "heroes" back bleeding with screamy mouths and weepy eyes! Oooo! Some limbs have been amusedly cleavèd! NOOO! The blasted clerics have prevented fatalities with their priggish priestly zeal.

Several clerics have retired for the evening already, their holy might spent.

But Bri'An furtively observes, prattling quietly of Tyr's graces. Is't too much to wish for ONE CORPSE?! For without the dead, I cannot send ANY on their journey. . . . Patience!

Meanwhile, Sasha is chewing off her fingers' nails in hunger.

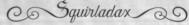

Squirladax

A yearning pang in my gutsack! It has been hours now, and my ribs quarrel with my brains. OK! I have made the executive decision to order a plate of Goldenstars and a single Onion Loaf. 'Twas the last of our coppers, but filling enough, and will perhaps staunch the greedy lips of my minions long enough for Bri'An to work his blasted miracle and for us to get paid!

I've come to wonder of Bri'An's powers. Although his faith is unquestioned, he has only laid hands to heal one of us . . . and it 'twas himself. However—I am reminded—he professed to feel much better after laying hands on he, Tyr be praised.

The wounded burble up from Undermountain bloody and babbling, and two more clerics have collapsed of exhaustion in their attempts to save the anguished heroes.

NOW! I call forth Bri'An to HEAL! But Bri'An bids me hold, for firstly he must limber up.

Not long, my sweet Ruby, 'til you shall be matriarch to a family of jewels and treasures.

ZOUNDS! SASHA HOWLS! Why now do tears spray from her eyes, why does she scrub at her wounds with sticks of salty butters. WHAT?! I DID NOT AUTHORIZE BUTTERS!

Deelia

Bri'An's warm-up blessings bless this unholiest of drinking holes, and still, no one has died. At this, I am sullen. . . . I am also very drunk. Dismay floods my sinking heart as I realize that **these last groups** returning may be my last hope at a bounty of freshly slain souls.

Squirladax screeches fiscally at young Sasha, while Bri'An plays DARTS!? This is torment! Let us heal these maggots and be OUT! Bri'An now cries out to the kitchen, something about a "Heroes' Feast."

Bri'An

By my honor, what happened was NOT MY FAULT! Here's how it played, on Tyr's honor.

The Heroes' Feast arrived. Clearly a gift from the house for faithful service. We did what Tyr bid when he lay his bounty before you. We feasted upon succulent, sandwich—like Talyth and the freshest of green Chopforest. The main course, that of the most blessed Hot River Crab Bites, followed by a most pious Laumberry Pie, served alongside Mingari-Spiced Owlbear Milk and a pastry that was sour of cream and made from the nuts of wal.

Sasha feasted the feast of warriors.

Deelia found a peace unknown to her cursed people in potent drink!

Our leader Squirladax sang goblin songs through sharp teeth, stippled with the finest meats and pastries!

AND I GAVE THIS! MY service here this night. . . . By Tyr's grace, of course.

Then the rickety squeals of the winch screeched my senses to sharpness as the elevated platform began its slow ascent! A cry, "Adventurers return . . . and with wounded!"

I . . . must guess . . . that some mechanical failing occurred with the winch and the platform plummeted to Undermountain.

I shall never forget their cries or their brave sacrifice. May Tyr greet them at his holy gates.

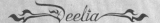

Deelia

WHAT HELL?! I keep replaying the events in my drink-addled brain. What I saw I could not have. Shortly before the winch broke, a flit of parchment appeared on our table. A bill—a wicked BILL. The cost, presumably, of the Heroes' Feast. Ne'er have I seen such want of coin, such greed, as that of the wretched BILL.

Bri'An and I locked eyes over this grave, unjust report. Then it was Squirladax's eyes that went wide as he shook his head and slipped Ruby back into his pouch. Not TWO, nor FIVE BUREAUS OF DARK TABLES could ever hope to pay off this bill.

I knew in that instant what must be done.

With a scream, I summoned all the powers of the Raven Queen and vaporized this ghastly receipt . . . with fire!

At the same moment, following what plan I know not, Bri'An drew his smiting hammer and shattered the winch in blind, shrieking panic!

For this I will not forgive him, for as Sasha and Squirladax bid us FLEE the Yawning Portal, I was robbed of my chance to collect what surely was a bounty of souls at the bottom of the well! Queen, forgive me!

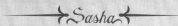

Sasha

I am so freaked out right now. An ambush! City Watch officers jumped out at us in an alley behind the Blackstar Inn! Squirladax shoved me back toward them screaming that I should "assume the front line." His heave knocked me into their grasping gauntlets! I thought for sure they had me, but their grabbing hands slipped off my heavily buttered limbs. I fled swiftly!

I'm breathing so heavy right now, guys, but you should have seen how fast I was! Anyways, while I have clearly improved speed and dexterity thanks to my butter treatment, it has become clear, as I gasp for breath, that my breath bellows are weak and need strengthening. There's a whole chapter on this in the *Volo's Guide*, and I have to work on this.

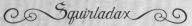

Squirladax

My shockèd goblin mind is racing, my lungs burn with the ill humors of exhaustion. We have been hiding in a Waterdeep sewer drain for nigh. . . . I do not know how long! The sun's rays peek over the rooftops as throngs of City Watch seek us! WHAT happened?! Bri'An isn't talking.

Running is hopeless. The Bureau's bellies are bursting of crustaceans and cheeses, and their sweat is as of gravy. I'd stop to ask them for council but their brains are bobbing in a wash of mead! I require time to plot our next move. . . . Wait! Bobbing in a wash! That's it!

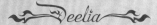

Deelia

I lurch about an unevenly planked floor. Squirladax, the foul rodent, beams above me with pride and boasts of our newfound "safety." The room in which I find myself is not safe! It is cursed with a swaying that roils the mead still sloshing in my guts.

Goblin "leader" Squirladax has funneled us to shelter in the hold of some ship, and the room spins. The wafting aroma of dead fish twists at my gorge. There is also the clanging of the City Watch bell that rattles my throbbing skull.

All I wish to know is, why in the Nine Hells was a Heroes' Feast ordered and why did we not sacrifice Ruby to pay for it?!

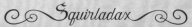

Squirladax

Deelia has confronted me about Ruby, and why she was not sacrificed to ransom us against our dangers. Ruby is not coin to be tossed aside. Ruby is the mother of future fortunes. Oh wait. Oh no! Wherefore art my beloved Ruby?! I sweep my pockets with goblin fingers and feel her naught!

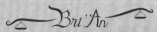

Bri'An

BY TYR'S GRACE, DO YOU HEAR THE CLING CLANGING STEPS ON THE PLANKS ABOVE US? The City Watch have found us! We are certainly doomed! DOOMED!

GOLDENSTARS

MAKES ABOUT 15 PASTRIES

DOUGH

2½ cups all-purpose flour

2 teaspoons granulated sugar

1 tablespoon onion powder

½ teaspoon baking powder

1 teaspoon kosher salt

½ teaspoon freshly ground
black pepper

2 eggs

½ cup neutral oil

¼ cup water

FILLING

1½ teaspoons neutral oil

One 4-ounce mild-flavored
fresh sausage, casing removed
(see Cook's Note, page 11)

¾ cup diced (about ⅜-inch cubes)
peeled Yukon gold potato

¼ cup water

Kosher salt

1 tablespoon unsalted butter

1¼ cups loosely packed very thinly
sliced leeks (white and light green
parts; halved lengthwise before slicing)

1½ teaspoons chopped fresh thyme

1½ tablespoons all-purpose flour

¾ cup low-sodium chicken broth

Freshly ground black pepper

¼ cup chopped fresh parsley

EGG WASH

1 egg

1 tablespoon water

As you step onto the docks of Berdusk, the Jewel of the Vale—perhaps fresh off one of the many boats that ply the River Chionthar—there's a good chance the first thing you'll eat will be a goldenstar. These rich little pastries, traditionally stuffed with a local chicken sausage and Goldenfields batatas and leeks, are known for their distinctive triangular shape. Vendors sell them everywhere, and their heartiness will tide you over until you can manage a sit-down meal. Varieties of the goldenstar have spread throughout the Sword Coast, from the river's end at Baldur's Gate to as far north as Neverwinter. But every time you eat one done right, you'll be brought back to the docks of Berdusk.

To make the dough: In a large bowl, combine the flour, sugar, onion powder, baking powder, salt, and pepper and whisk together. In a medium bowl, combine the eggs, neutral oil, and water and whisk until uniform. Add the wet mixture to the dry mixture and, using a flexible spatula, fold until incorporated into a dough.

Turn the dough onto a work surface and knead briefly until it comes together. Divide in half and pat each half into a roughly 6-inch disc. Place the discs side by side in the bowl or on a plate, cover with a kitchen towel, and let rest for about 1 hour.

To make the filling: Line a small plate with a paper towel and set aside.

In a medium nonstick skillet over medium heat, warm the neutral oil. Add the sausage and cook, stirring and breaking it into small crumbles, until it no longer appears raw, about 3 minutes. With a slotted spoon, transfer the sausage to the prepared plate, leaving as much of the rendered fat in the skillet as possible.

Return the skillet to medium heat. Add the potato, water, and 1 pinch salt and cook, covered, stirring occasionally to prevent sticking, until the potato starts to soften, about 6 minutes. Add the butter and let melt, swirling to coat the pan. Add the leek, thyme, and 1 pinch salt and cook, stirring, until softened, about 2 minutes. Add the flour and cook, stirring constantly, for 2 minutes. Slowly add the chicken broth, stirring constantly and scraping the bottom of the skillet to dissolve the browned bits, and cook until thickened, about 1½ minutes (the texture will be quite thick, almost like loose mashed potatoes). Add the reserved sausage and stir to incorporate. Remove the skillet from the heat and let the mixture cool until barely warm, 10 to 15 minutes. Taste and adjust the seasoning with additional salt and pepper, if necessary. Stir in the parsley. CONTINUED →

*Fresh sausages come in a variety of
sizes and flavors. Choose a mild flavor
such as spinach or roasted garlic and
steer clear of strong, spicy, or smoky
flavors. Turkey sausage is fine here, if
you prefer it.*

*If you don't have a 4-inch round
cookie or biscuit cutter, you can use a
small dish 4 inches in diameter with
a thin rim to cut the dough rounds.*

*A bench scraper is a useful and
inexpensive tool. You can use it to level
flour in a measuring cup, or batter in
a baking pan, in addition to loosening
dough from a work surface.*

*Goldenstars can be wrapped in
aluminum foil and refrigerated for up
to 4 days. Before serving, reheat in a
350°F oven, still wrapped in foil, until
warmed through, about 30 minutes.*

GOLDENSTARS CONTINUED

With racks in the upper- and lower-middle positions, preheat the oven to
375°F. Line two baking sheets with parchment paper or nonstick baking
mats, and set aside.

To make the egg wash: In a small bowl, whisk the egg and water until
uniformly yellow. Set aside.

On a generously floured work surface, roll out one of the dough discs
into a roughly 12-inch circle no more ¼ inch thick. Using a 4-inch round
cookie or biscuit cutter, cut out four or five rounds. Gather the dough
scraps into a mass, return to the bowl or plate, and cover.

If necessary, use a bench scraper to gently loosen the dough rounds from
the work surface. Place about 1½ tablespoons of the filling in the center
of each round. Lightly brush the edges of each round with the egg wash.
Working with one at a time, form a triangle by folding three "sides" up
and over the filling, leaving about 1 inch of filling uncovered. Pinch the
edges together well (so they won't come apart as they bake). Place on a
prepared baking sheet, about 2 inches apart.

Clean the work surface, if necessary, flour it generously, and repeat the
process with the second dough disc, rolling the dough, cutting, filling,
shaping, and sealing the rounds. Add the collected scraps to those from
the first disc.

Clean the work surface, if necessary. Knead the collected dough scraps
into a cohesive mass, pat it into a roughly 6-inch disc, cover, and let
rest for about 15 minutes. Flour the work surface generously, and roll
out, cut, fill, shape, and seal about five to seven final rounds. Transfer
the pastries to the prepared baking sheets. Brush the three sides of the
pastries (but not the exposed filling) with egg wash.

Bake the goldenstars until light golden and the filling is bubbling, about
25 minutes, swapping and rotating the baking sheets halfway through. Let
the pastries cool on the baking sheets for about 5 minutes, then transfer
them to wire racks and let cool until barely warm or room temperature
before serving.

TALYTH

MAKES ABOUT 30 SANDWICHES

1¾ cups all-purpose flour

1½ cups finely grated aged
Asiago cheese

1½ tablespoons onion powder

1½ tablespoons minced fresh thyme

1 tablespoon cornstarch

1½ teaspoons kosher salt

1 teaspoon freshly ground black pepper

1 pinch cayenne pepper

8 tablespoons very cold unsalted
butter, cut into 16 slices

¼ cup whole milk

One 4-inch piece summer sausage,
sliced ⅛ inch thick on a slight diagonal
(see Cook's Note)

COOK'S NOTES

*When slicing the sausage, trim as
necessary so the diameter is a little
smaller than the 2½-inch diameter
of the dough, to ensure the slices fit
together nicely.*

*If you prefer, you can substitute
another type of fully cooked sausage,
such as Portuguese-style chouriço.
Avoid cured, dried styles of sausage,
which can turn leathery and tough
as the talyth bake.*

The palm-size sandwich known as talyth is a beloved appetizer on many a menu, from Waterdeep and the rustic watering holes of Luskan to the cloistered refectories of Candlekeep and eateries as far east as the Sea of Fallen Stars where, it is said, the dish originated. Although countless variations exist, talyth commonly comprises meats (typically sliced sausage), cheese, spices, and herbs nestled between two large crackers, all lightly baked to adhere the layers. While the baking process seals in flavor, it also ensures its portability, making talyth a common travel snack along the major Faerûnian trade routes. Although frozen talyth can easily be reheated on an open campfire, freshly made talyth affords a more eclectic and adventurous array of savory ingredients, including diced egg, oysters, snails, and even spiced worms.

In a food processor, combine the flour, cheese, onion powder, thyme, cornstarch, salt, black pepper, and cayenne and process for about 15 seconds. Scatter the butter slices over the flour mixture and pulse to cut the butter into the flour until the mixture has the texture of wet sand, about twelve 3-second pulses. With the motor running, add the milk through the feed tube and process until a dough just comes together, about 30 seconds (do not overprocess).

Transfer the dough to a work surface and knead, if necessary, a couple of times to bring it together. Divide the dough in half, and roll each half into a log measuring about 2½ inches in diameter and 3 inches long. Wrap each log with plastic wrap and refrigerate until very firm, at least 2 hours or up to 3 days.

With racks in the upper- and lower-middle positions, preheat the oven to 350°F. Line two baking sheets with parchment paper or nonstick baking mats, and set aside.

Unwrap the dough logs and, using a serrated knife, cut into thirty ¼-inch-thick rounds, giving them a quarter turn between each cut to help preserve the cylindrical shape. Arrange them on the prepared baking sheets about ½ inch apart. Place one slice of sausage onto each slice of dough, pressing to help it adhere.

Bake the talyth until lightly browned around the edges and on the bottom, 24 to 28 minutes, swapping and rotating the baking sheets halfway through. Remove the sheets from the oven and, working quickly, use the underside of a dinner fork to gently press the sausage slices again so they adhere to the dough. Let the talyth cool on the baking sheets to room temperature before serving.

CHOPFOREST

SERVES 4 TO 6

1 pound green cabbage, finely shredded

Kosher salt

¼ cup Kalamata olives, pitted and finely chopped

1 tablespoon white balsamic vinegar

1½ teaspoons finely grated lemon zest

1 teaspoon pressed or grated garlic

Freshly ground black pepper

3 tablespoons extra-virgin olive oil

1 medium fennel bulb, trimmed, cored, and thinly sliced, plus about 1½ tablespoons chopped fronds

4 medium scallions, trimmed; whites thinly sliced and greens cut into ½-inch lengths

⅓ cup chopped fresh parsley

COOK'S NOTE

You can substitute thinly shaved fresh brussels sprouts for some or all of the cabbage if you'd like. It will decrease the yield a bit, as brussels sprouts leaves are more delicate than cabbage, and they compact more once dressed. If you use shaved brussels sprouts, there's no need to salt and rest them.

Many examinations of early Yawning Portal menus have noted that its heavy, often greasy, fare had a celebratory "last meal" sense about it. This is likely because return from the Undermountain was simply not expected, with only the soiled dishware of stout adventurers left behind. However, as more adventurers survived the mad mage Halaster's labyrinth, the menu evolved to accommodate a balance of healthier options. Senior cook Jarandur Tallstand adapted the traditional wood-elven forest salad, or chopforest, as it has been called, to complement the heavier menu options with its mix of peppered leaves, olives, fennel, and tangy vinaigrette dressing. It is said that a chopforest delivered unto your table, compliments of Yawning Portal proprietor and Undermountain gatekeeper Durnan, is a happy omen before one's descent to Undermountain.

In a colander or large strainer set over a medium bowl, toss the cabbage with 2 teaspoons salt. Let the cabbage rest until slightly wilted, at least 1 hour or up to 4 hours. Rinse the cabbage well under very cold running water, drain thoroughly, and dry very well with a clean kitchen towel or paper towels. Scrape the cabbage into a large bowl and fluff it with your fingers (it can be covered and refrigerated for up to 3 days).

Meanwhile, in a large bowl, combine the olives, vinegar, lemon zest, garlic, and ½ teaspoon salt; season with pepper; and whisk to incorporate. While whisking vigorously, add the olive oil in a slow, steady stream to combine and emulsify into a dressing.

Add the cabbage, fennel bulb, scallions, and parsley to the bowl and toss to combine. Adjust the seasoning with additional salt and pepper, if necessary, and sprinkle with the fennel fronds before serving.

Hot River Crab Bites

SERVES 4

6 ounces high-quality crabmeat
(see Cook's Note), drained

1 tablespoon fresh lemon juice,
plus 2 teaspoons finely grated
lemon zest (see Cook's Note)

½ teaspoon kosher salt

Freshly ground black pepper

¼ cup crème fraîche

⅓ cup finely chopped fresh chives

2 endives, root ends trimmed
and larger outer leaves separated
(see Cook's Note)

COOK'S NOTES

*Some markets sell freshly picked
crabmeat in the seafood department
or containers of pasteurized crabmeat
in a refrigerated case near packaged
smoked salmon, herring, and
other fish. Both are more flavorful
choices than the canned crabmeat
you may find near the canned tuna
and sardines.*

*Zest the lemon before squeezing the
juice, as it's easier to zest intact fruit.*

*In case you're not familiar with
endive, they are small, pale, torpedo-
shaped heads of lettuce (really, a type
of chicory) with a pleasant, mildly
bitter flavor. If you can't find or don't
like endive, you can serve the crab on
crackers, cucumber slices, or lightly
toasted slices of baguette.*

A center of music and the arts, the town of Berdusk, in Faerûn's western heartlands, is known for many things, but above all for its hot river crabs. A specialty of the Sign of the Silver Sword Inn, these river delicacies are as dependent on freshness as on seasoning. Traditionally, locals would harvest crabs with soft shells and consume them within the day. As for the crab recipe, it's a closely guarded secret, but is believed to include crème fraîche and lemon zest mixed into a spread and served on endive. At only one copper piece per plate, they'll leave enough in your coinpurse for a glass of Saerloonian Glowfire—the perfect complement.

Blot the crabmeat dry with a paper towel, if necessary, and pick over for shell fragments. Transfer to a small bowl, and add the lemon juice and ¼ teaspoon of the salt; season with pepper; and stir to incorporate. Add the crème fraîche, lemon zest, remaining ¼ teaspoon salt, and most of the chives; season with additional pepper; and stir gently to mix. Taste and adjust the seasoning with additional salt and pepper, if necessary.

Scoop about 1 tablespoon of the crab mixture into each of sixteen endive leaves, arrange them on a platter, and sprinkle with the remaining chives. Serve immediately.

SORNSTAG

SERVES 4

¼ cup fine breadcrumbs

2 tablespoons extra-virgin olive oil

4 garlic cloves; 2 peeled and left whole, 2 pressed or grated

½ cup slivered almonds

2½ pounds venison chuck or rump, cut into 1½-inch pieces

Kosher salt and freshly ground black pepper

About 4 teaspoons neutral oil

2 large yellow onions, chopped

2 bay leaves

2 teaspoons minced fresh thyme, or 1 teaspoon dried

½ teaspoon ground cinnamon

⅛ teaspoon ground cloves

¾ cup dry red wine

¾ cup low-sodium chicken broth

1 teaspoon cocoa powder (preferably Dutch-processed)

⅔ cup chopped fresh parsley

Popular at holiday gatherings of humans and elves alike, sornstag is a simmered venison dish that can be seasoned and prepared in a variety of ways. Traditional elven sornstag is slow smoldered with ground coriander, cumin, and hotspice or curry in a thick broth and is a popular plate among wood elves during the Highharvestide Festival. Humans have also adopted their own stewed preparation techniques for this gamey, yet succulent, main course. Throughout the wooded regions of Faerûn, stags are hunted by humans for both sport and meal, resulting in the proliferation of venison-based cuisine. In the bucolic forests and fields of the Dalelands, the most popular regional recipe for sornstag demands a full day's preparation. The traditional recipe calls for powdered almonds simmered with red wine to form the emulsified base of a piquant sauce, in which the meat soaks overnight before it is slow-cooked on an open flame from dawn for an early evening feast. But to get it to the table faster, you can skip the overnight marinade and cook it in an oven for just a few hours. Notably, the Silver Taproom, in Essembra, sees travelers from far and wide eager to sample its famous pied sornstag, which consists of a heaping ladle of this venison stew baked inside a buttery crust. You'll know the sornstag pies are ready when the scent of the aromatic pastry wafts down bustling Rauthauvyr's Road.

Line a plate with paper towels.

In a large sauté pan or Dutch oven over medium heat, toast the breadcrumbs, stirring constantly, until fragrant and a shade darker, about 3 minutes. Scrape the breadcrumbs into a small bowl, and carefully wipe out the pan.

Add the olive oil and whole garlic to the pan, return it to medium heat, and cook, undisturbed, for 1 minute. Add the almonds and cook, stirring constantly, until browned and fragrant, about 1 minute (be vigilant, as they can burn quickly). With a slotted spoon, scoop the almonds and garlic onto the prepared plate to drain. Add the garlic and ⅓ cup of the almonds to the breadcrumbs; reserve the remaining almonds separately. Pour the oil from the pan into a small bowl and set aside. Carefully wipe out the pan.

Sprinkle the venison all over with 1½ teaspoons salt and 1 teaspoon pepper. Set the pan over medium-high heat, add 2 teaspoons of the neutral oil, and warm until shimmering. Add about one-third of the venison, so the pieces are close together in a single layer, but not touching, and cook, undisturbed, until well browned on the bottom, about CONTINUED →

SORNSTAG CONTINUED

2 minutes. Turn the pieces and cook, undisturbed, until the second side is well browned, about 2 minutes longer. Transfer the venison to a large bowl. Repeat to brown the remaining meat in one or two batches, adding more oil if needed, and adjusting the heat as necessary to avoid scorching. Transfer to the bowl with the first batch.

Set the sauté pan over medium heat, add the reserved olive oil, and allow it to warm for a moment. Add the onions, bay leaves, thyme, and ½ teaspoon salt and cook, stirring and scraping the bottom of the pan to loosen any caramelized bits, until softened, about 6 minutes. Add the pressed garlic, cinnamon, and cloves and cook, stirring, until fragrant, about 40 seconds. Add the wine, adjust the heat to medium-high, and bring to a strong simmer, again scraping the bottom of the pan to loosen any caramelized bits. Add the chicken broth and venison with any accumulated juices, stir to combine, and return to a strong simmer. Cover the pan, adjust the heat to medium-low to maintain a bare simmer, and let simmer until the venison is tender, about 2 hours.

Using a small liquid measuring cup or mug, scoop about ½ cup of the cooking liquid from the pan. Add the cocoa powder and stir until uniform. Pour the cocoa mixture back into the pan, add ½ teaspoon salt and ½ teaspoon pepper, and stir to combine.

With the same measuring cup or mug, scoop another ½ cup of cooking liquid from the pan and transfer to a blender. Add the reserved breadcrumb-almond mixture and about ¼ cup of the parsley and blend until the nuts are pulverized and the mixture is thick and very smooth, about 1 minute, stopping to scrape down the sides of the blender jar at least once during that time. Scrape the mixture into the pan, stir to combine thoroughly, and partially cover the pan. Continue to cook, stirring and scraping the bottom of the pan occasionally, until the stew is thickened, 15 to 25 minutes longer. Remove the bay leaves if desired, add about ⅓ cup parsley, and stir to combine. Adjust the seasoning with additional salt and pepper, if necessary. Divide the sornstag among individual bowls, sprinkle each with a few of the reserved toasted almonds and some parsley. Serve immediately.

ROTHÉ STEAK

SERVES 4

Two 1-pound boneless strip steaks
(see Cook's Note), 1½ to 2 inches thick

Kosher salt and freshly ground
black pepper

1 tablespoon neutral oil

3 tablespoons unsalted butter

2 garlic cloves, crushed and peeled

8 large sprigs fresh thyme
or rosemary

COOK'S NOTES

Cast iron is the skillet of choice here because it retains heat so well.

This cooking technique is a bit messy—the fat splatters in the intense heat, and a splatter screen is of no help because of the frequent turning. The entire process moves fast, so turn on your exhaust fan and have your tongs, basting spoon, and thermometer at hand before you start cooking. And, of course, use oven mitts when handling the screaming-hot skillet.

Depending on where you live, strip steak may be called shell steak, sirloin strip steak, New York strip steak, Kansas City strip steak, or Texas strip steak, among other names. Whatever name it goes by, make sure it's thick.

A large-flake, crunchy salt, like Maldon, is a terrific finish at serving time.

One silver piece is an extraordinary bargain for the Rothé Steak at the Yawning Portal—even if it is one of the more expensive things on the menu. Served sizzling-hot right out of the skillet, with just a hint of garlic and garden spices, rothé steak is a carnivore's delight and the perfect protein for a triumphant or aspiring adventurer. Along the Sword Coast, you can easily source fresh rothé that is either farm-raised or wild game—there are devotees of both. Why bother with any vegetable sides? You won't get to them with this slab of meat to tackle.

⊃⊏⬦⊐⊂

Using paper towels, pat the steaks dry and season generously with salt and pepper on both sides and along the edges. Place the steaks on a plate and let rest at room temperature for 1 hour. (Or refrigerate, loosely covered, for up to 2 days. Return the steaks to room temperature before cooking.)

Set a large cast-iron skillet over medium heat for 7 minutes (the pan may smoke a bit). Adjust the heat to high, add the neutral oil, and swirl to coat the bottom of the pan (the oil will smoke too). Add the steaks and cook, flipping them every 30 seconds, until a pale golden crust begins to form on both sides, 3 to 4 minutes.

Adjust the heat to medium-high, slide the steaks to one side of the skillet, add the butter to the other side, and allow it to melt and foam slightly. Add the garlic and thyme to the butter. Tilt the pan toward the butter so that it pools opposite the steaks and, while continuing to flip the steaks every 30 seconds, use a long-handled, large metal spoon to baste them with the butter and aromatics, concentrating on spots that are lighter and less crusted. (If the butter smokes or the steaks begin to burn, lower the heat slightly.) Cook, basting and flipping the steaks, until an instant-read thermometer inserted into the thickest spot registers 120° to 125°F for medium-rare, about 7 minutes longer, or about 130°F for medium, 8 to 9 minutes longer.

Transfer the steaks to a carving board, tent loosely with aluminum foil, and let rest for 10 minutes. Slice the steaks against the grain into roughly ½-inch-thick slices before serving.

Onion Loaf

MAKES ONE 9-INCH LOAF

5 tablespoons unsalted butter

1½ teaspoons neutral oil

1 medium yellow onion, chopped

Kosher salt

1 small leek (white and light green parts), halved lengthwise and thinly sliced

2 cups whole-wheat flour

1 cup all-purpose flour

1½ tablespoons onion powder

2½ teaspoons baking powder

¼ teaspoon baking soda

2 eggs

1 tablespoon light brown sugar

¾ cup buttermilk

¾ cup thinly sliced scallions (white and green parts)

COOK'S NOTES

An oval baking dish helps the loaf keep an oblong, grublike shape as it bakes and expands.

Some of the onion mixture will burn in the dish and may stick to the bottom of the loaf, but you can just brush off any burnt bits.

The onion loaf can be wrapped tightly in plastic wrap and stored at room temperature for up to 2 days.

The onion loaf on the menu at the Yawning Portal is done in the Cormyr style: big, dark loaves, as dense as the King's Forest. While the onion may be the headliner, the real stars of the show are the leeks, scallions, and fresh buttermilk, which help round out the flavors of this rich, crusty loaf—perfect for morningfeast or eveningfeast. When it's time to break bread with adventuring companions, old and new, an onion loaf is an inexpensive and delicious option that's practically a meal in itself.

With a rack in the middle position, preheat the oven to 375°F.

In a small skillet over medium heat, melt 1 tablespoon of the butter with the neutral oil. Add the onion and ¾ teaspoon salt and cook, stirring occasionally, until the onion is translucent and starting to soften, about 3 minutes. Add the leek and cook, stirring occasionally, until softened, about 3 minutes longer. Scrape the mixture into a bowl and set aside to cool.

Return the skillet to medium heat and melt the remaining 4 tablespoons butter. Remove from the heat and pour about 1 tablespoon of the melted butter into a 10- to 11-inch oval gratin dish (preferably enameled cast iron). With a pastry brush, coat the inside of the dish with the butter and set aside. Reserve the remaining melted butter in the skillet.

In a large bowl, combine both flours, the onion powder, baking powder, baking soda, and 1¼ teaspoons salt and whisk together. In another large bowl, whisk together the eggs and brown sugar. Add the buttermilk to the egg mixture and whisk to combine. Add the dry mixture and, using a flexible spatula, fold and stir until nearly incorporated. Add the reserved melted butter and the scallions and continue to fold and stir until all the ingredients come together to form a lumpy dough. Knead a couple of times in the bowl, if necessary.

Scrape the dough into the prepared dish, shape into an 8-inch log, and spread the reserved onion mixture evenly over the top and sides, pressing into the dough to help it adhere.

Bake the loaf until it is firm to the touch on top, a toothpick inserted into the center comes out clean, and the onion mixture on the surface is browned with some crisp edges, 45 to 50 minutes, rotating halfway through. Let cool in the gratin dish for about 10 minutes, then transfer the bread to a wire rack to cool to room temperature. Slice with a serrated knife before serving.

SOUR CREAM–WALNUT CAKE

MAKES ONE 8-INCH
SQUARE CAKE

TOPPING

⅓ cup all-purpose flour

¼ cup granulated sugar

¼ cup packed light brown sugar

½ teaspoon ground cinnamon

¼ teaspoon kosher salt

⅔ cup walnut pieces, toasted lightly
(see Cook's Note) and cooled

5 tablespoons unsalted butter,
melted and cooled

1 cup walnut pieces, toasted lightly
and cooled

2 cups all-purpose flour

2½ teaspoons instant espresso powder

1½ teaspoons baking powder

½ teaspoon baking soda

¾ teaspoon ground cinnamon

1 teaspoon kosher salt

2 eggs

1 cup sour cream

½ cup neutral oil

1½ teaspoons vanilla extract

½ cup granulated sugar

⅔ cup packed light brown sugar

COOK'S NOTES

*To toast nuts or seeds, warm a heavy
skillet over medium heat until hot. Add
the nuts or seeds and spread out in a
single layer. Cook, stirring constantly,
until they are fragrant and as brown
as desired.*

*The cake can be wrapped tightly
in plastic wrap and stored at room
temperature for up to 2 days.*

It's rare to see this halfling specialty on the table, usually because it's gone before you ever catch a glimpse of it. Perfect for morningfeast, or teatime, the much-celebrated sour cream–walnut cake includes a delicious crumble of cinnamon, brown sugar, and walnuts, but it's the cake itself that takes the cake. A recipe passed down orally by generations of halflings, it is said to be made with the finest Luiren grain flour, fresh sour cream, and finely ground kaeth or coffee. The only known issue with the pastry is that there never seems to be enough of it.

To make the topping: In a food processor, combine the flour, both sugars, cinnamon, and salt. Scatter the walnuts on top and drizzle the melted butter over the mixture. Pulse until the mixture just begins to resemble a wet, coarse sand, about three 2-second pulses (do not overprocess and pulverize the nuts). Scrape the mixture onto a plate (no need to clean the work bowl, as you'll use it again) and refrigerate for 20 minutes.

With a rack in the middle position, preheat the oven to 350°F. Coat an 8-inch square baking pan with nonstick cooking spray and set aside.

In the food processor, pulse the walnuts with ¼ cup of the flour until the walnuts are coarsely ground, about five 2-second pulses. Pour the walnut mixture into a medium bowl; add the remaining 1¾ cups flour, the espresso powder, baking powder, baking soda, cinnamon, and salt; and whisk to combine.

In a large bowl, whisk the eggs until uniform. Add the sour cream, neutral oil, and vanilla and whisk vigorously to combine. Add both sugars and again whisk vigorously to combine. Add the flour mixture and, using a flexible spatula, fold to blend the wet and dry ingredients just until no pockets of dry ingredients remain. Scrape the batter into the prepared pan, and smooth the top.

Working quickly, with your fingers, sprinkle the topping evenly over the surface, forming pea- to hazelnut-size clumps. Gently pat the topping onto the batter to help secure it.

Bake the cake until the top is lightly browned and a toothpick inserted into the center comes out clean, 40 to 45 minutes, rotating the pan about halfway through. Transfer to a wire rack and let cool to room temperature before cutting and serving.

LAUMBERRY PIE

MAKES FOUR 5-INCH PIES

2 frozen piecrusts (for one double-crust pie), thawed according to the package directions until cooler than room temperature and pliable

7 cups mixed fresh blackberries and blueberries, rinsed and very gently dried with paper towels

½ to ⅔ cup granulated sugar (depending on the berries' sweetness)

3½ tablespoons cornstarch

¼ teaspoon kosher salt

1 tablespoon fresh lemon juice

½ teaspoon vanilla extract

⅓ cup apple or red currant jelly

1 cup fresh raspberries, rinsed and very gently dried with paper towels

COOK'S NOTE

You'll need four 5-inch pie plates.

The Yawning Portal of Waterdeep serves a new pie every week, based on the seasonal ingredients available. You're really in luck when laumberries from the frosty Frozenfar are in season. Their tartness is softened by the sweetness of the dough, making it the perfect blend of flavors. The famous tavern likely pilfered the idea from the hardy bakers of Bryn Shander. Pies in this style are made off-season with blueberries, blackberries, and raspberries, which together give you something of the flavor of the original. They're best served a bit chilled, and when done right have been known to resurrect the spirits of weary adventurers emerging from the Undermountain.

On a floured work surface or sheet of parchment paper, roll out one of the piecrusts into an oval about 14 inches long and 7 inches wide. Cut out two 7-inch circles of dough and fit each into individual 5-inch pie plates. Fold under any overhanging dough to be even with the edge of the rim. Place your thumb and index finger on the folded edge of crust and press between them with the index finger of your other hand. Work your way around the crust in this manner to create a decorative wavy rim. Repeat with the second piecrust. Cover the dough-lined plates with plastic wrap and place in the freezer for about 30 minutes.

With a rack in the middle position, preheat the oven to 350°F.

Place the partially frozen dough-lined plates on a rimmed baking sheet. Line the doughs with aluminum foil, and fill with pie weights, making sure there are enough to reach most of the way up the sides.

Bake the crusts until the edges are set and just beginning to turn golden, 25 to 30 minutes, rotating the baking sheet halfway through. Carefully remove the foil and weights and continue baking until the crusts are light golden brown and crisp, about 12 minutes longer, again rotating the baking sheet halfway through (cover the edges of the crusts with foil if they begin to darken too much). Transfer the piecrusts to a wire rack and let cool to room temperature.

Place 2 cups of the mixed blackberries and blueberries in a medium bowl and set aside.

In a food processor, puree the remaining 5 cups mixed blackberries and blueberries until broken down and smooth, about 1 minute. Strain the puree through a fine-mesh strainer into a medium nonreactive saucepan (such as stainless steel), scraping and pressing on the solids to extract as much puree as possible, and scraping the puree off the bottom of the strainer into the saucepan. In a small bowl, combine CONTINUED →

LAUMBERRY PIE CONTINUED

½ cup sugar, the cornstarch, and salt and whisk to incorporate; then whisk that mixture into the berry puree. Taste and add the remaining sugar, if necessary.

Set the saucepan over medium heat and bring the berry mixture to a strong simmer, stirring and scraping the pan bottom constantly. Cook until the mixture is thickened and pudding-like and bubbles start to break the surface, about 20 minutes. Remove the saucepan from the heat, add the lemon juice and vanilla, and whisk to combine. Let the puree cool slightly.

Meanwhile, in a small saucepan over medium heat, warm the apple jelly until runny, stirring to smooth out lumps. Drizzle the melted jelly over the reserved blackberries and blueberries and toss gently to coat. Add the raspberries and toss very gently to coat and mix with the other berries.

Scrape one-fourth of the slightly cooled berry puree into each cooled piecrust, and top each with ¾ cup of the glazed fresh berries. Loosely cover the pies with plastic wrap. Refrigerate until chilled and the puree has set, about 3 hours or up to 1 day, before serving.

MINGARI-SPICED OWLBEAR MILK

MAKES ABOUT 4 CUPS

½ cup old-fashioned oats

1 cup water

4 cups milk (see Cook's Note), plus more as needed

2½ tablespoons granulated sugar

1½ tablespoons light brown sugar

1 pinch kosher salt

3 cinnamon sticks, plus ground cinnamon for sprinkling

While conventionally prepared with a base of owlbear milk, other types of milk such as yak milk, buttermilk, rice milk, and even nut milk are all suitable substitutes in this creamy, cozy concoction. But no matter which milk you choose, there is no alternative for Mingari spice, culled from the inner bark of Mingari trees. Likened in both flavor and scent to cinnamon, Mingari spice is a rare but highly sought-after seasoning indigenous to southeast Faerûn. Although rare, this strong, aromatic spice is incredibly versatile, at home in both sweet and savory dishes, and thus it has spread throughout the Realms and beyond. However, satisfying Mingari-Spiced Owlbear Milk requires merely a dash of this scarce but potent accent. Travelers in search of a day starter, an alcohol-infused night capper, or even a medicinal stomach soother, invariably relish a tall mug of this nourishing milk.

In a dry medium saucepan over medium heat, toast the oatmeal, stirring constantly, until very fragrant, 4 to 5 minutes (take care to avoid burning it). Remove from the heat, add the water (it will spatter), and gently swirl the pan. Add the milk, both sugars, salt, and cinnamon sticks and stir to mix. Return the pan to medium heat and bring to a low, steamy simmer, stirring often, about 7 minutes. Adjust the heat to low and continue to simmer, stirring occasionally, until cooked through and soft, about 5 minutes. (If the mixture threatens to boil over, remove the pan from the heat until the foam recedes and then continue.) Remove the pan from the heat and let the mixture cool to room temperature. Scrape into a large wide-mouth jar with a tight-fitting lid, seal, and refrigerate until well chilled, at least 4 hours or up to 24 hours.

Remove the mixture from the refrigerator. Remove and reserve the cinnamon sticks. Scrape the mixture into a blender (keep the jar handy) and blend on high speed until as uniform and smooth as possible. Strain through a fine-mesh strainer back into the jar, working it with a flexible spatula until just a couple of teaspoons of oat paste remain. Discard the paste, return the cinnamon sticks to the jar, cover, and refrigerate until cold, about 1 hour.

Remove the jar from the refrigerator and vigorously shake it. Adjust the consistency of the mixture, if desired, by adding up to ¾ cup milk, ¼ cup at a time, shaking after each addition to blend. Remove the cinnamon sticks and pour the milk into glasses (over ice, if desired). Sprinkle each with ground cinnamon before serving.

COOK'S NOTE

Any type of milk—from skim to whole—is fine, depending on how rich a drink you want. If you fancy a light, tangy drink, substitute ⅓ cup buttermilk for the same amount of regular milk.

NEVERWINTER NECTAR

MAKES ABOUT 1¾ QUARTS

2 large juicy oranges, scrubbed

1 large juicy lemon, scrubbed

3 tablespoons granulated sugar

1 cup apple juice

½ cup brandy

One 750 ml bottle inexpensive white wine, chilled (not oaked; see Cook's Note)

1 apple, washed well

1 cup seltzer, cold

1 cup small ice cubes, plus more for serving

COOK'S NOTE

Good choices for the white wine include dry Riesling, Gewürztraminer, Grüner Veltliner, Pinot Grigio (or Gris), or Sauvignon Blanc. Wines with oaky notes aren't great here, so steer clear of Chardonnay, which may or may not be oaked.

Neverwinter nectar is an expensive but tasty spirit-based drink, known for its sweet fruit-infused flavor, buttery base, and citrus-tinged aftertaste. Perennially popular in Neverwinter, this "nectar" has gradually appeared on the drink lists of many of the finer eateries among the well-traveled cities of the Sword Coast. The surprisingly crisp and refreshing cocktail is so rich in flavor, it is often consumed in lieu of dessert or as an accompaniment to lighter fare. Veteran barkeeps unlock the full spectrum of flavors when they combine the unique mixture of juices, brandy, and white wine with a touch of sparkling water and ice. Felzoun's Folly, in Waterdeep, serves one of the more notable iterations of this syrupy and perfectly divine concoction.

Quarter one of the oranges and the lemon, cutting them from the stem end to the blossom end. Cut the quarters crosswise into thin slices and place in a sturdy container. Add the sugar, stir, and set aside until the fruit softens a little, about 20 minutes. Using a potato masher, muddler, or wooden spoon, mash and muddle the mixture until the fruit releases its juice, the skins are bruised, and the juices and sugar become syrupy. Add the apple juice, brandy, and wine; stir; then cover and refrigerate for at least 4 hours or up to 24 hours.

Set a fine-mesh strainer over a large bowl. Strain the mixture, using a sturdy spoon to press on and work the solids to exude as much liquid as possible. Discard or compost the solids and pour the liquid into a serving pitcher. Quarter the remaining orange, again cutting from the stem end to the blossom end, and thinly slice the quarters crosswise. Add to the pitcher. Quarter and core the apple, and thinly slice the quarters crosswise. Add to the pitcher, along with the seltzer and ice cubes and stir to blend. Serve over ice.

Butternut Beer

SERVES 2

Large ice cubes

3 ounces rye or bourbon

1½ ounces butterscotch schnapps

2 teaspoons fresh lemon juice

6 drops bitters (such as Angostura)

4 ounces plain seltzer, cold

8 ounces cream soda, cold

2 lemon slices

COOK'S NOTE

To frost the mugs, put in the freezer for an hour before using.

As most adventurers know, there are serious spirits, hard liquors, and courage-enhancing brews that serve to bolster one's resolve before a trip down the well into the Undermountain. The drink known as butternut beer is none of these things. Instead, it is a sweetened and mirthful beverage best served as a dessert for a hearty meal or after a long day's night exploring Halaster's lair. Although it packs enough bourbon and butterscotch schnapps to rattle the senses, it is not intended to impair judgment. Rather, it's meant to encourage a hearty belly laugh and dull the aches of an adventurer's knotted muscles.

Fill two frosted mugs about halfway with ice. To each, add 1½ ounces rye, ¾ ounce schnapps, 1 teaspoon lemon juice, and 3 drops bitters and stir to blend and chill. Add 2 ounces seltzer and 4 ounces cream soda to each mug, and again stir gently to blend.

Garnish each drink with a lemon slice before serving.

THE ROCK OF BRAL

After escaping an exorbitant bill at the YAWNING PORTAL,
our heroes bravely fled the City of Waterdeep aboard a SPELLJAMMER.
Hurtled through time and space to the mysterious ROCK OF BRAL,
the Bureau is charged with a QUEST!"

Squirladax

So, the oddest event has befallen us.

Some hours after we fled the Yawning Portal—cause of an unpaid bill—we found sanctuary in the underhold of a sea vessel docked at port. As I calmed my stalwart party, a door creaked aside, and framed in dim light came to us a small, curious figure—no taller than my brother, had I one. Encased head to toe in dented bronze plate, squat and pot-bellied, this ancient lad called out in a fluty gasp.

"ARE YOU THE QUATERNATE TETRAD?"

As all wise adventurers know, when someone asks you if you are who you are NOT, you say YES.

So, I did thus. "Yes! Of course we are."

Satisfied, he answered me in rusty reverberance: "I am DINT, Autognome (what 'tis?) and captain of the Dashor (what 'er means that!), and we are running behind! Please produce the Jewel of Javanium."

And to this I answered, "We have that . . . not."

Bronzèd Dint tilted his head, the armored eye-slits narrowing. Just then, I could hear the shout of City Watch grow closer.

"Are you not the Quaternate Tetrad? As ordered?"

Bri'An called out, "By Tyr, what is to be won if we are?!"

Dint's rusty flute-voice grew in conspiracy, "Why, five Astral Diamonds, of course."

It was then that Bri'An, to my great shock, produced Ruby—my precious Ruby!—from a hidden flap in his holy vestments, and presented it thusly to Dint, who responded by swallowing Ruby whole! NO! Dint's eye-slits glowed red for a moment before he turned and withdrew from view. . . . And with a mighty groan, our vessel set sail.

I cast an incredulous eye to Bri'An who assuaged me with pious honesty that Ruby was rescued from the ground when she slipped from my leathers as we fled.

Thus, Ruby is safe, though INSIDE the gut of our strange new companion. What purpose does she serve in this bronze-armored gnome's trunk?!

The sweeping sway of the boat lulls me as I surrender to exhaustion.

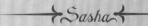

Sasha

OH MY GODS! Guys! So, I went above decks. . . or to the abovedecks? Whatever, I'm not nautical! Anyways, I snuck up there to do some training. As I peeked out over the stairwell,

I spied that squat little bronze guy hoisting the jibs—or jibbing the hoists, whatever! Boat stuff!—until mighty, multicolored sails flexed above me. Beyond them was the craziest sky I'd ever seen; it was like breathtaking moonlight mixed with burning sunsets! WOW!

So, as I totally had questions, I stepped up to the above-deck, and FROZE. Glancing over the side of our boat . . . I could see . . . NO SEA! Only an endless sky. A little freaked out now, I paged through *Volo's Guide* to the section on "Accidental Death & Dismemberment."

Oh CRAP! WE DIED! And this . . . must be the AFTERLIFE!

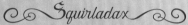

Squirladax

Intrepid reader and observer of the Bureau of Dark Tables. As life goes, I have good news and—its shadowy twin—bad news. I shall start with the good news, nay, the BEST news. There is NO afterlife! Therefore I can only conclude that we are alive! The bad news? We are sailing a bewildering sea of stars toward a free-floating mountain in the sky.

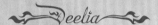

Deelia

Foolish bard! Squirladax blusters that there is no afterlife—how I grow eager to show him! There is most certainly an afterlife, a "Shadowfell," and THIS NOT BE IT, heathens. I questioned the Ow-Toe-Gnome Dint and have concluded that we are aboard an object known as a SPELLJAMMER. Passingly familiar with such legends, I know it to be a ship that sails the endless space between spaces. I know not where this vessel is headed, but I fear that we have jumped from the frying pan into the fire.

Squirladax

'Tis the best day of my life! We have anchored at the dizzying Rock of Bral, and Dint has relayed to me our purpose in this Realmspace metropolis sited upon a disclike asteroid. Repeat. Dint has a PURPOSE for us! A QUEST! And a REWARD for the questing. FIVE ASTRAL DIAMONDS! And, while I do not know what an Astral Diamond is worth, I do suspect that five such diamonds are worth easily FIVE TIMES as much!

We are to proceed with great covertness into the Rock of Bral's High City district, blending into the teeming throngs of bizarre creatures from myriad realms. It is at the upscale Man-o-War restaurant overlooking Lake Bral that we shall broker a deal with a barkeep known as Jack the Knife for a rare bottle of wine: Veneno 1318 DR.

For this purpose, Dint has supplied us with 200 gold pieces to exchange for the Veneno, which he assured me should be more than enough by twice!

I shall now utter words of bardic magic to the Bureau to inspire brilliant execution of our tasks.

Heed not peril, nor flame, nor fiery ends,
For wax that wanes drips through the cracks.
And if that wax shall whack thee back,
A seal of greatness upon your slacks.
You wear the pants of your own destiny, my friends.

Deelia

Squirladax has again "inspired us" with his poetry. I've heard more inspirational things coming from the Yawning Portal's outhouse.

Bri'An

I have advised it is Tyr's wisdom that we split the party, along with the gold, so as to double our chances of success! Squirladax agrees. I have taken young Sasha under my wing. She bid that I keep my sharp dragoneyes open for a supply of live leeches, and thus I seek these. However, Tyr's holiest crap! The Tamarind Balls and Loaf Pudding in the Great Market are prodigious. Seriously. Alas, a miracle of flavors sent straight from Tyr!

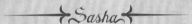
Sasha

Great news! Bri'An has returned with the leeches! Per the instructions from *Volo's Guide to Bodily Health*, I have applied Bri'An's leeches to my temples as a means of cooling my overhot head, allowing me to "stay cool under the pressures of combat." Bri'An has also purchased Lake Bral Smoked Herring and Steaks of the Deep, which, once eaten, will improve my swimming and breath bellow capacity. I'm going to be in the best shape of my life! We eat! As do the leeches!

Deelia

As I wander this floating ball of mud with Squirladax, my brain shrinks as the "Goblin Poet" barrages me with castigations regarding previous failures. He is obsessed!

"I need you to casteth spells of great destruction upon our enemies," he spittles! Of course, he knows nothing from whence my power was forged. Nothing of the furnaced heats of Shadow's Edge Academy, nor its Lords who smelted my very soul.

I've always known my life would be cleavèd short, but now I know by whom.

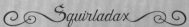
Squirladax

After a happy confabulation with Deelia concerning strategerie, we are arrivèd at the Man-o-War, indeed a place of high society . . . and extraordinary foods! After sampling the Tavern Noodles and a crispy skewerèd fish dish called the Tears of Selûne (to blend in), we finally made contact with Jack the Knife. A mightily tall, barrel-chested orc in a smock of chain mail—charming fellow, he! The Veneno '18 taunts me from its place of honor behind the bar on the highest shelf, and it could already have been mine this instant, were it not for. . . . WAIT! Greedy meanderings!

Our pious cleric Bri'An has spent down our moneys! To load down his draconic paunch, n'doubt! When I ask for reasonings from him, all I receive in return is a drunken burble that smelt of expensive Undermountain Alurlyath drink!

This is inexcusable! We are on a QUEST!

As we HAD twice the moneys, now reduced to but half the moneys needed, I must devise a solution. Think, Squirladax, think! THAT'S IT! I shall use charismatic diplomacy to charm the price of the Veneno '18 by HALF! Brilliant! Now where is Jack the Knife?!

Strange. There he be, behind the bar . . . but squatter, rounder, and decidedly less orcish . . . more draconic than I remember.

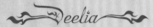

It is nothing short of remarkable how we have managed to turn a simple wine purchase into a . . . I'm not even sure what this is.

Bri'An bet me I couldn't choke out that Jack the Knife guy. Ha! I showed him. It wasn't easy as he almost slipped out of my buttered arms, and I only pray that his stiff neck will benefit from the effects of the butter treatment when he awakes. Wait. Why is Bri'An stripping him bare?

TYR be PRAISED! I have braised the beefs of success this day with the gravy of cleverness. 'Tis Tyr that whispered thusly to me. Said he, "Bri'An. Bri'An, my most devout. Hammer thy kitchen staff to unconsciousness with thy sap. Bring thy chainmail smock of Jack the Knife to thy chin and wear'st thou so that thy identity be transformèd to that of he who is chokèd by holy sister Sasha." And whence he dropped out from under Sasha's buttered embrace, so did I do'st this thing Tyr commanded me.

Disguised thusly as Jack of the Knife, I reached—in plain sight of all—for thy sweet bottle of Veneno '18.

But alas, Tyr granted me strength, but not arm length-th.

So then did I LEAP, and a great CRASHING of bottles and glass did crunch beneath my sandaled feet! But Veneno. . . . Ah! I seized Veneno to mine bosom.

It was then that a fountain of flame spewed forth from the hands of Deelia causing the patrons to cower beneath tables.

"TYR, GUIDE ME," I called out!

And it was in that moment that much purifying fire washed over the Man-o-War. Was this of right or wrong, who can say? But Tyr granted me speed as I fled the cindered cries!

Tyr be praised. I am parched!

I was trying to incinerate Bri'An for his blundering incompetence, but alas, he is dragonborn and more than a bit fire resistant.

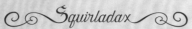

My bardic tongue is speechless. It has been an hour since our return to the Dashor and our return to this crazy wild . . . space. I will now hand this quill over to Dint for I shall be damned to repeat what I just witnessed.

· · · · · · · Dint · · · · · · ·

Hello! I am Dint. I am repeating what he just witnessed. Why is this Veneno freshly uncorked? Why are there dribbles of red wetness on the tabard of the dragonborn? Did one of you drink this?

Veneno is poisonous to all but the undead.

Fried Soy with Vegetables

SERVES 4

One 14- to 20-ounce block firm or extra-firm tofu

3 tablespoons soy sauce

2½ tablespoons Shaoxing rice wine or dry sherry

3 teaspoons toasted sesame oil

⅓ cup low-sodium chicken broth, vegetable broth, or water

1 teaspoon light brown sugar

1 teaspoon cornstarch

6 medium scallions, white parts minced and green parts cut into 1-inch lengths

1½ tablespoons minced or grated fresh ginger

1 tablespoon minced or grated garlic

¼ cup neutral oil

Three 3-ounce baby bok choy (about 5 inches long), trimmed at the base and quartered lengthwise

2 medium carrots, peeled and cut into 2-inch matchsticks

1 large red bell pepper, cored, seeded, and cut into ½-inch-wide strips

Kosher salt and freshly ground black pepper

COOK'S NOTE────────────

Serve this with hot freshly cooked rice—brown or white.

This soy-based protein dish originated from a gnome recipe, but it is equally popular with those who shy away from animal meat, including some communities of elves. It is also ideal in environments where livestock is harder to keep, such as the Underdark and the Rock of Bral. The original gnome version uses chicken broth as a base, but vegetable broths work just as well. While the tofu is the star, the mélange of scallions, bok choy, bell pepper, and carrots imparts a variety of textures and flavors. Rice-based cooking wine and soy sauce make it a lustrous and savory meal.

Line a small baking sheet or cutting board with a clean kitchen towel or triple thickness of paper towels. Halve the tofu block lengthwise, cut each half into 1-inch-thick slices, and arrange on the prepared baking sheet. Top the tofu with another clean kitchen towel or triple thickness of paper towels and a second baking sheet or small cutting board. Weight it down with a large skillet or pot (or something of similar weight) and set aside to drain for 20 minutes.

On a large shallow dish, arrange the pressed tofu slices in a single layer. In a small bowl, combine 1 tablespoon of the soy sauce, 1 tablespoon of the rice wine, and 1½ teaspoons of the sesame oil and whisk to incorporate. Pour over the tofu, turn the slices to coat (take care not to break them), and let marinate for 15 minutes, turning them again halfway through.

Meanwhile, in a small bowl, combine the remaining 2 tablespoons soy sauce, remaining 1½ tablespoons rice wine, remaining 1½ teaspoons sesame oil, the chicken broth, brown sugar, and cornstarch; whisk to blend; and set aside. In another small bowl, combine the scallion whites, ginger, garlic, and 2 teaspoons of the neutral oil; stir to incorporate; and set aside.

In a large nonstick skillet over high heat, warm 2 teaspoons neutral oil until shimmering. Tilt the skillet to coat the bottom, add the tofu in a single layer, and cook, undisturbed, until browned on the bottom, 2½ to 3½ minutes. Turn the slices and continue cooking until browned on the second side, 2½ to 3½ minutes longer. Transfer the tofu to a large bowl, cut the slices in half, if desired, and set aside.

Return the skillet to high heat, add 2 teaspoons neutral oil, and warm until shimmering. Tilt the skillet to coat the bottom, add the bok choy, cut-side down, sprinkle lightly with salt, and cook, undisturbed, until spotted with brown on the bottom, about 2 minutes. Turn the pieces so the second cut side is down and continue to cook, CONTINUED →

FRIED SOY WITH VEGETABLES CONTINUED

undisturbed, until that side is spotty brown and the bok choy is barely tender, about 2 minutes longer. Transfer to the bowl with the tofu.

Return the skillet to high heat, add 2 teaspoons neutral oil, and warm until shimmering. Tilt the skillet to coat the bottom; add the carrots, bell pepper, and ¼ teaspoon salt; and cook, stirring occasionally, until barely tender, about 2 minutes.

Adjust the heat to medium, clear the center of the skillet, add the remaining 4 teaspoons neutral oil, and allow it to warm for a moment. Add the ginger-garlic mixture and cook, stirring and mashing the mixture, until fragrant, about 45 seconds. Whisk the soy sauce mixture to recombine, add to the skillet, and cook, stirring constantly, until the sauce is thickened, about 45 seconds.

Add the tofu, bok choy, scallion greens, and ½ teaspoon salt to the skillet and season with pepper. Cook, stirring constantly, until heated through and coated with sauce, about 1 minute. Divide among four plates and serve immediately.

Tavern Noodles

SERVES 4 TO 6

⅓ cup extra-virgin olive oil

3 large onions, halved from pole to pole and thinly sliced lengthwise

Kosher salt

1½ teaspoons minced fresh rosemary or thyme

2 teaspoons pressed or grated garlic

½ cup dry white wine

12 ounces fettuccine, tagliatelle, or pappardelle

¾ cup grated Parmesan, plus more for serving

Freshly ground black pepper

⅓ cup chopped fresh parsley

3 hard-cooked eggs, peeled and chopped

While the flavorful plate simply known as tavern noodles is a common dish throughout the multiverse, the version on offer in the various watering holes across the Rock of Bral is truly otherworldly. The noodles themselves are rumored to be the mouth tentacles of the catfish found in the deepest depths of Lake Bral. The truth of this is impossible to ascertain. What's less obscure is how delicious this dish is, especially when drenched in a light sauce made with rosemary, garlic, onion, and white wine, as they do at the Man-o-War restaurant in the Rock of Bral's High City. Whether by magic or mischief, these noodles are sure to satisfy even the most space-weary explorers.

In a medium nonstick skillet over medium heat, warm 3 tablespoons of the olive oil until shimmering. Add the onions and 1 teaspoon salt and cook, stirring frequently, until soft and light gold, about 30 minutes. Add the rosemary and 1 teaspoon of the garlic and cook, stirring, until fragrant, about 40 seconds. Add the wine, adjust the heat to medium-high, and cook, stirring occasionally, until the liquid is reduced by half, about 2½ minutes.

While the onions are cooking, in a large pot over high heat, bring 4 quarts of water to a boil. Add 1 tablespoon salt and the fettuccine and cook, stirring occasionally to prevent sticking, until just barely al dente. Reserve 1 cup of the cooking water. Drain the pasta and return it to the pot. Adjust the heat to medium-low, add the onion mixture to the pasta, toss, and cook, stirring constantly, for 1 minute. Remove the pan from the heat, add the remaining 2 tablespoons plus 1 teaspoon olive oil, remaining 1 teaspoon garlic, the Parmesan, and 1 teaspoon salt. Season with pepper and toss well. Add between ½ cup and 1 cup of the reserved cooking water to loosen the sauce and distribute the ingredients evenly. Add most of the parsley and toss. Adjust the seasoning with additional salt and pepper, if necessary, and transfer the pasta into a serving dish. Sprinkle with the chopped egg and remaining parsley before serving.

TAMARIND BALLS

MAKES 18 TAMARIND BALLS

6 ounces tamarind pulp
(see Cook's Note)

¼ cup tightly packed, quartered
pitted dates (quartered lengthwise)

¼ cup granulated sugar, plus more
as needed

½ teaspoon vanilla extract

1 pinch kosher salt

3 tablespoons large-crystal sugar
(such as Turbinado or Demerara)

COOK'S NOTES

*Rectangular blocks of tamarind pulp
are available at many international
markets. Often the package says that
the pulp is seedless, but that's not
always the case. Make sure there are
no seeds before adding the pulp to the
food processor.*

*Large-crystal sugar, such as Demerara,
Turbinado, or Trader Joe's organic
cane sugar, makes a particularly pretty
coating, but you can certainly use
regular granulated sugar.*

For those seeking sugary baubles to brighten the palate, do not neglect the sour yet sweet tamarind balls that festoon the market stalls of Trademeet and the areas surrounding Firedrake Bay in the lands of Faerûn. From Amn to Calimshan to Tashalar, these tasty morsels made of tamarind pulp and dates are a much beloved dessert and trail-side snack. Some of the finest examples exist a few miles to the south of Trademeet in Mosstone, at the venerable Drover's Last Drink, where they add a bit of vanilla and large-crystal sugar to the mix. These treats travel well, and spelljammer captains docking at Baldur's Gate have brought them to the Rock of Bral and beyond, where they are much sought after by astral elves, giff, and even space clowns.

Using your fingers, break up the tamarind pulp into very small bits, feeling for whole seeds or large fragments and removing any that you discover. Transfer to a food processor or mini chopper. Add the dates, granulated sugar, vanilla, and salt and process or chop until the ingredients are combined and very finely chopped, 30 seconds to 1 minute. Transfer the mixture to a small bowl.

Place the large-crystal sugar in a wide, shallow bowl. Roll 2-teaspoon portions of the tamarind mixture into eighteen scant 1-inch balls, gently pressing as you roll to help them cohere. Working with three or four balls at a time, roll them in the crystal sugar, pressing gently to help it adhere. Store in an airtight container at room temperature for up to 4 days.

TRENCHER BREAD

MAKES FOUR 10-INCH FLATBREADS

2 cups whole-wheat flour

¾ cup all-purpose flour, plus more for dusting

¼ cup stone-ground cornmeal

2½ teaspoons kosher salt

2½ teaspoons baking powder

½ teaspoon baking soda

1¼ cups whole milk or low-fat Greek yogurt (not nonfat)

⅓ cup extra-virgin olive oil

3 tablespoons neutral oil

COOK'S NOTE

Brushing the breads with extra-virgin olive oil or melted butter while they're still warm is a nice touch.

Predating even the most rustic plates, trencher bread served as a functional, and edible, tool for serving food. Usually allowed to harden and become stale, this flat, round loaf can not only hold the meal but also become the next course once the edible "plate" has absorbed any juices or sauce and softened. Even when civilization along the Sword Coast advanced, the pre-Netherese tradition of serving food on edible plates remained. No longer used for pure utility, trencher bread is traditionally prepared hard, flat, and dry, but it is lightly salted and seasoned to make the "second course" more appealing. It has also taken on other shapes, notably a bowl, which has become a popular vessel for serving soups and stews. The bread is served along the crowded, cobbled lanes of major metropolises as far south as Calimport and as distant as the Rock of Bral asteroid spaceport. Look for street vendors in Middle City's Great Market serving rare mammalian meats and sauces on this bread—a quick and cheap option for on-the-move off-worlders—and embrace the novelty of an ancient taste of Toril.

Lightly flour a work surface. In a large bowl, combine the whole-wheat flour, all-purpose flour, cornmeal, salt, baking powder, and baking soda and whisk to incorporate. Make a well in the center, add the milk and olive oil, and, using a wooden spoon or your hands, stir around the perimeter of the well to incorporate the dry ingredients into the wet (the dough will look a little rough and shaggy). Scrape the dough onto the prepared work surface and knead until smooth and uniform, dusting with a tiny amount of all-purpose flour as you go if the dough becomes too sticky. Divide the dough into four equal portions. Gently roll each portion into a ball, cover with a clean kitchen towel, and let rest for 15 minutes.

Preheat the oven to 125°F.

Using a rolling pin, roll out one of the dough balls into a circle with an 11-inch diameter. In a 12-inch heavy skillet (preferably cast iron) over medium heat, warm about 2 teaspoons of the neutral oil until hot. Tilt the skillet to coat the bottom with oil, carefully place the dough circle in the skillet, and cook, undisturbed, until spotted with brown on the bottom and slightly puffed, 3 to 4 minutes. Turn the round over and continue to cook, undisturbed, until the second side is spotty brown as well, 3 to 4 minutes longer. Transfer the bread to a baking sheet or ovenproof plate and place it in the oven to keep warm. One at a time, roll and cook the remaining rounds, adding the remaining 1 tablespoon neutral oil and adjusting the heat if necessary to avoid burning, and transferring them to the oven keep warm. Serve immediately.

Tears of Selûne

SERVES 4

⅓ cup mirin

3 tablespoons sake

3 tablespoons soy sauce

2 tablespoons granulated sugar

1 teaspoon smoked paprika (optional)

1½ pounds firm white fish fillets (such as sea bass), cut into roughly 1-inch cubes

2 tablespoons neutral oil

Hot freshly cooked rice for serving

1 large scallion (white and light green parts), thinly sliced

1 tablespoon sesame seeds, lightly toasted (see Cook's Note, page 24) and cooled

The bustling pedestrian pathways that etch the Rock of Bral are known for their prodigious offerings of finger foods. One such treat that garners all the accolades from the "locals" is a dish called the Tears of Selûne, a spicy, spit-roasted crispy fish, which came into fashion as a quick, crunchy snack that you can eat off a stick. Typically made with a firm white fish, like sea bass, the secret weapon of these delicacies is said to be the seasoning—a tantalizing mix of paprika, soy sauce, and sesame seeds. Today, you can sample these crispy treats throughout the Rock of Bral. Some street chefs fry them in a skillet, though connoisseurs insist the open flame yields the best texture. Whichever way you cook them, these fish skewers are best served with a starchy base, such as warm rice, to help all the delectable textures and savory flavors go down just right.

In a medium skillet over medium heat, combine the mirin, sake, soy sauce, sugar, and paprika (if using) and bring to a steamy simmer, swirling the skillet to dissolve the sugar. Once a few bubbles form around the edges, continue simmering, swirling the pan occasionally, until tight, glossy, foamy bubbles cover most of the surface, about 5½ minutes. Remove from the heat and let the mixture cool until just warm and thickened to the consistency of a loose glaze, 5 to 6 minutes.

Preheat the grill to medium-high.

Thread the cubed fish onto metal or pre-soaked bamboo skewers. Drizzle with oil and gently turn to coat. Once the grill is hot, cook the fish skewers until cooked through and lightly charred, 6 to 8 minutes, turning them over halfway through cooking. Just before removing the fish from the grill, gently brush it all over with the glaze.

Spoon a portion of rice onto each of four serving plates or bowls. Arrange the fish skewers over the rice, then sprinkle each portion with the scallions and sesame seeds. Serve immediately.

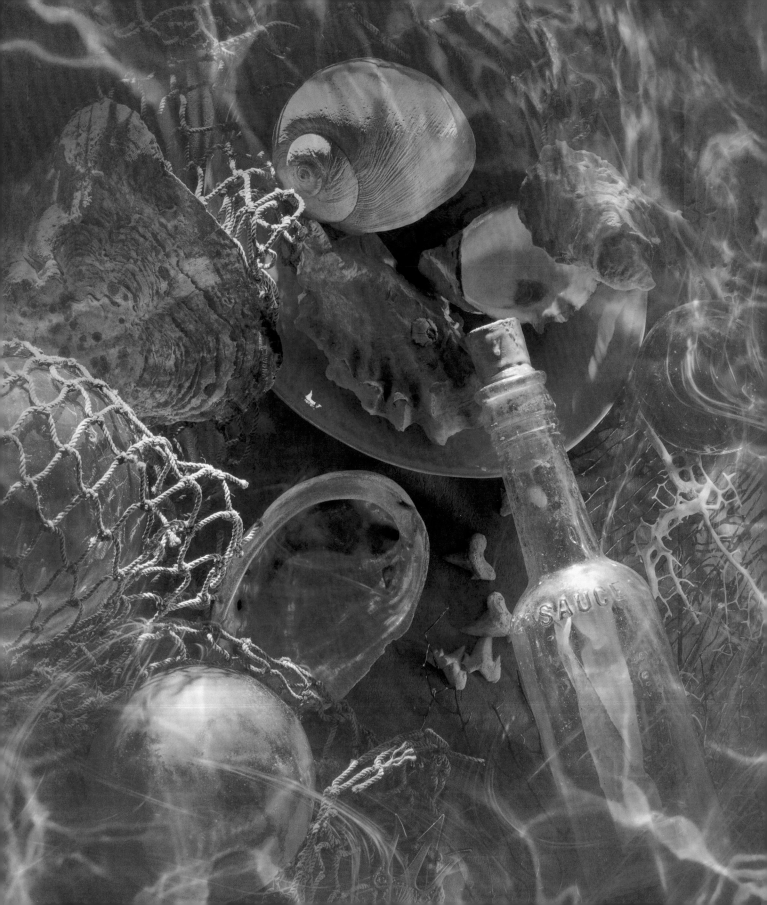

DUERGAR SMOKED HERRING

SERVES 4

1½ tablespoons neutral oil or extra-virgin olive oil

1 medium yellow onion, chopped

1 red bell pepper, cored, seeded, and chopped

1 Cubanelle pepper or a small green bell pepper, cored, seeded, and chopped

1 Scotch bonnet or habanero chile, pricked all over with a fork

Kosher salt

1 tablespoon tomato paste

2 teaspoons minced fresh thyme

1 teaspoon pressed or grated garlic

4 plum tomatoes, cored and chopped

Three 3.25-ounce tins smoked kipper snacks, drained

6 scallions (white and green parts), thinly sliced

1 tablespoon fresh lime juice, plus lime wedges for serving

Freshly ground black pepper

COOK'S NOTE————————

Sliced avocado and sliced hard-boiled egg are nice accompaniments. This easily becomes a full meal when served with rice and a salad.

To many duergar, dwarves of the Underdark, food is simply the nourishment needed to get back to work. But the duergar are also renowned craftsmen, and what they do, they do well, which includes cooking a small but reliable menu of staples. And perhaps no duergar food is more prized than their smoked herring. While the original boasts herring from the dangerous depths of Darklake, known for imbuing the fish with distinctive brine and mineral flavorings, this version utilizes herring sourced from bountiful Lake Bral, a vital repository of water located in the center of this well-populated asteroid. There is no denying that a proper subterranean brine takes especially well to heat from Underdark fire lichen, but chile peppers will suffice for those chefs cooking on the surface. A specialty of the duergar enclave at the Underdark trading post of Mantol-Derith, this maritime delicacy is much sought after, from far below the surface of Toril all the way to the otherworldly Rock of Bral.

In a large skillet over medium heat, warm the neutral oil until shimmering. Add the onion, red bell pepper, Cubanelle pepper, Scotch bonnet, and 1 teaspoon salt and cook, stirring frequently, until softened, about 5 minutes. Add the tomato paste and cook, stirring, until fragrant and a shade darker, about 1½ minutes. Add the thyme and garlic and cook, stirring until fragrant, about 40 seconds. Add the tomatoes and cook, stirring occasionally, until they begin to soften, about 3 minutes. Add the kippers and cook, stirring occasionally and taking care not to completely shred the fish (though it will break down some as you stir, which is fine), until heated through, about 3 minutes longer. Add most of the scallions and the lime juice and season with black pepper, stirring to incorporate.

Remove the skillet from the heat and discard the whole chile. Adjust the seasoning with additional salt and pepper, if necessary. Serve immediately, sprinkling each portion with some of the remaining scallions and a lime wedge on the side.

SPICED PORK AND ORANGE PEPPERS

SERVES 4

½ teaspoon paprika

½ teaspoon ground coriander

½ teaspoon ground fennel

½ teaspoon garlic powder

¼ teaspoon ground cumin

⅛ teaspoon cayenne pepper
(or more if you like it hot)

Kosher salt and freshly ground
black pepper

1 large pork tenderloin (1½ pounds),
silverskin removed (see Cook's
Note, page 54), and patted dry with
paper towels

3 tablespoon extra-virgin olive oil

1 large yellow onion, halved from pole
to pole and sliced lengthwise

4 large orange bell peppers, cored,
seeded, and cut into ¾-inch-wide strips

5 garlic cloves, thinly sliced

1 tablespoon chopped fresh thyme

2 teaspoons sherry, cider, or wine
vinegar, plus more as needed

⅓ cup chopped fresh parsley

It is said, "When in space, do as spacefarers do," and this can prove useful advice when talking about food. One will never know how, or why, pork became such a readily available source of protein on the Rock of Bral, but that mystery is beside the point when a steaming bowl of spiced pork and orange peppers is on offer. In truth, the underside of the one-mile-long ovaloid asteroid, founded by humanoid Captain Bral, serves as a sustainable and farmable ecosystem capable of oxygen production. It even contains a freshwater lake (Lake Bral), frequently refilled by water harvested from ice asteroids, and, yes, livestock in the form of swine. Spiced Pork and Orange Peppers was a favorite of the famed Captain Bral and has remained a signature dish on the menu of the Laughing Beholder, run by gregarious beholder Large Luigi, and other notably unsavory eateries that dot the avenues of this lawless asteroid outpost. When ordered "the Captain's way," the explosion of spices (paprika, coriander, cayenne, garlic, fennel, cumin, and some mystery space seed grown onsite) combined with the zest of the orange peppers is like a peg-legged dohwar kick straight to the taste buds.

With a rack in the middle position, preheat the oven to 425°F.

In a small bowl, combine the paprika, coriander, fennel, garlic powder, cumin, cayenne, ³/₄ teaspoon salt, and ³/₄ teaspoon black pepper and stir to incorporate. Rub the pork with 1 tablespoon of the olive oil, then sprinkle the spice mixture all over the meat, rubbing it into the surface.

In a large ovenproof skillet over medium-high heat, warm 1 tablespoon olive oil until shimmering. Add the pork, adjust the heat to medium, and cook until browned all over, giving it a quarter turn every 1½ minutes (adjusting the heat as necessary if the pan drippings threaten to scorch) until all four sides are cooked, about 6 minutes total. Transfer the tenderloin to a plate and set aside.

Return the skillet to medium heat, add the remaining 1 tablespoon olive oil, and let warm for a moment (taking care not to scorch the caramelized bits left in the skillet). Add the onion, bell peppers, and 1 teaspoon salt and cook, stirring and scraping the bottom of the skillet with a wooden spoon to release the caramelized bits as the vegetables release moisture, about 5 minutes. Continue cooking until the vegetables just begin to soften, about 3 minutes longer. Add the garlic and thyme and cook, stirring, until fragrant, about 1 minute longer. Return the pork to the skillet, positioning it over the vegetables. CONTINUED ➤

SPICED PORK AND ORANGE PEPPERS CONTINUED

Place the skillet in the oven and roast the meat until the center registers 140°F on an instant-read thermometer, 12 to 17 minutes, turning the tenderloin over midway through cooking. Transfer the tenderloin to a carving board, cover loosely with aluminum foil, and let rest until the pork reaches an internal temperature of 145° to 150°F, 5 to 10 minutes.

Meanwhile, turn off the oven and return the skillet with its vegetables to the oven to keep warm.

When the meat has almost finished resting, remove the skillet from the oven. Stir in the vinegar and most of the parsley. Taste and adjust the seasoning with salt and pepper, then scrape the vegetables onto a serving platter. Cut the pork on the diagonal into slices about ½ inch thick and arrange them over the vegetables. Sprinkle lightly with salt, pepper, and the remaining parsley before serving.

COOK'S NOTE

Silverskin is a light-colored (silvery) membrane on the meat that contracts when cooked. It can be removed with a sharp paring knife.

KELVIN & HUGHES
LONDON
1917

...& SPECIALLY DESIGNED FOR NAVIGATION
...RUMENT WITH A GRADUATED...AND IS FAIRLY LARGE
...ARTING WITH THE HELP OF VERNIER ARC OF BRASS
...N THE INDEX MIRROR READINGS CAN BE TAKEN
...TO 130.IN

Steak of the Deep

SERVES 4

⅓ cup extra-virgin olive oil, plus more for drizzling

1 medium yellow onion, chopped

1 bay leaf

Kosher salt

3 garlic cloves, thinly sliced

1½ teaspoons paprika

½ cup Amontillado or Fino sherry, plus 2 teaspoons

One 14½-ounce can petite-diced tomatoes

Freshly ground black pepper

1½ pounds swordfish steak, about 1 inch thick

¼ cup chopped fresh parsley

COOK'S NOTE

If the sauce cools to room temperature and becomes too thick and sticky, set the pan over medium-low heat until it's warm and viscous again.

According to legend, this hearty seafood steak was first prepared by homesick triton folk living among surface dwellers and eager for a nostalgic taste of their undersea home. Guardians of the deep, commonly clustered around ocean trenches and far from the eyes and reach of humankind, triton have increasingly emerged from self-imposed isolation to cohabit with the other peoples of the multiverse. A satisfying synthesis of tastes that borrows more from the surface world than from the seafloor, steak of the deep features a thick slab of braised swordfish, topped with a simmered tomato-based blend of onion, garlic, paprika, and a crisp dry sherry, yielding a fragrant and filling main course. While you won't find this in many triton settlements proper, it is a mainstay meal for well-traveled triton and is increasingly available at larger coastal taverns and, occasionally, the more far-flung spaceports of Realmspace.

In a braising pan or large sauté pan over medium heat, warm the olive oil. Add the onion, bay leaf, and ½ teaspoon salt and cook, stirring, until the onion starts to soften, about 3 minutes. Add the garlic and paprika and cook, stirring, until fragrant, about 1 minute longer. Add the ½ cup sherry, adjust the heat to medium-high, and bring to a strong simmer. Let simmer, stirring, for about 1 minute. Add the tomatoes and ¾ teaspoon salt and season with pepper. Return to a simmer and cook, stirring, to blend the flavors, about 3 minutes.

Sprinkle the swordfish on both sides with salt and pepper and nestle it into the tomato mixture. Adjust the heat to low, cover, and cook until the swordfish is opaque, just firm to the touch, and registers 130°F on an instant-read thermometer, about 25 minutes, turning it over halfway through cooking. Transfer the swordfish to a serving platter, leaving the sauce in the pan. Tent the fish loosely with aluminum foil, and let rest for about 5 minutes.

Meanwhile, adjust the heat to medium-high and bring the sauce to a strong simmer. Add most of the parsley and the remaining 2 teaspoons sherry, and stir to blend. Adjust the seasoning with additional salt and pepper, if necessary.

Top the swordfish with the tomato sauce, drizzle with olive oil, and sprinkle with the remaining parsley before serving.

Green Ice Rime

SERVES 4

½ teaspoon neutral oil

4½ cups 1% or 2% milk

3 envelopes unflavored gelatin
(2 tablespoons plus ¾ teaspoon)

⅓ cup granulated sugar

1 small pinch kosher salt

2 teaspoons mint extract

¼ teaspoon vanilla extract

3 small drops green food coloring

COOK'S NOTE

Glass or ceramic baking pans are your top choices here. Since you'll be cutting the gelatin right in the pan, you could easily damage the nonstick coating in a metal pan.

These chilly, wobbly, delicious squares of bright green jelly have become popular anywhere the people of the multiverse might need a refreshing and whimsical dessert, including the Rock of Bral where the natural refrigeration of Realmspace makes preparation a cinch. They are most often served in saucers on a bed of ice to keep them the ideal temperature. They have been nicknamed "the Gelatinous Cube" by some adventurers and there are confectioners who will suspend little candy swords or shields in the mix as a crunchy surprise that hits you right in the sweet tooth. The best part is that Green Ice Rime dissolves in your tummy . . . not the other way around.

Using a paper towel, spread the neutral oil in an 8- or 9-inch square baking pan, coating the bottom and sides and leaving a slight film. Set aside.

Pour 1½ cups of the milk into a wide bowl, sprinkle the gelatin evenly over the surface, and allow to soften, about 10 minutes.

In a medium saucepan over medium heat, warm the remaining 3 cups milk, the sugar, and salt, stirring to dissolve the sugar, until warm to the touch, about 7 minutes. Remove from the heat, add the gelatin mixture, and whisk until the gelatin dissolves. Let cool for about 10 minutes. Add the mint extract, vanilla, and food coloring and stir to incorporate. Pour the mixture into the prepared baking dish and refrigerate until firm, about 4 hours and no more than 2 days.

When ready to serve, cut the gelatin into 2-inch squares and transfer to chilled dessert goblets or sundae dishes.

Loaf Pudding

**MAKES ONE
8½ BY 4½-INCH LOAF**

LOAF

1⅓ cups all-purpose flour

⅔ cup almond meal

2 teaspoons baking powder

½ teaspoon kosher salt

8 tablespoons unsalted butter, at room temperature, cut into chunks

¾ cup granulated sugar

3 eggs

1 teaspoon vanilla extract

½ teaspoon almond extract

½ cup plain yogurt (preferably whole-milk)

3 tablespoons sliced almonds

SYRUP

¼ cup granulated sugar

3 tablespoons water

1 small pinch kosher salt

½ teaspoon vanilla extract

¼ teaspoon almond extract

COOK'S NOTES

A bamboo skewer is ideal for poking holes in the loaf.

The loaf has a fragile crumb, made more so by the syrup, so use a serrated knife to slice it as neatly as you can.

The Elfsong Tavern of Baldur's Gate is known for many things: the disembodied singing voice of an elven maiden for which the tavern is named; the stuffed baby beholder over the mantle; and the driftglobe-lit taproom. But there is no better reason to visit this famous haven for adventurers than its delectable Loaf Pudding. A specialty of halfling head-chef Chenna Fatrabbit and her human pastry sidekick, Klav Martilmur, this moist, yogurt-infused loaf is soaked in a delicious vanilla-almond syrup and topped with a sprinkle of salted almonds to add just the right amount of crunch. The dessert is so coveted that even Spelljammer pirates have occasionally dropped into port to bring a loaf or two back to Realmspace.

To make the loaf: With a rack in the middle position, preheat the oven to 350°F. Coat an 8½ by 4½-inch loaf pan with nonstick cooking spray and set aside. Line a rimmed baking sheet with parchment paper or a nonstick baking mat, place a wire rack on top, and set aside.

In a medium bowl, combine the flour, almond meal, baking powder, and salt; whisk to incorporate; and set aside.

In the bowl of a stand mixer fitted with the paddle attachment, or with a handheld mixer, on medium-high speed, beat the butter and sugar until pale and fluffy, about 3 minutes, stopping to scrape down the sides of the bowl with a flexible spatula once or twice. Add the eggs, one at a time, beating well after each addition. Add the vanilla and almond extract, beat well, and scrape down the sides of the bowl again.

Adjust the mixer speed to low. Add about one-third of the flour mixture, followed by half of the yogurt, mixing after each addition until just incorporated, about 5 seconds. Repeat with half of the remaining flour mixture, followed by all the remaining yogurt. Scrape down the sides of the bowl again and add the remaining flour mixture. Adjust the speed to medium-low and mix just until the batter is smooth (do not overmix).

Using a flexible spatula, scrape the batter into the prepared loaf pan, smooth the top, and sprinkle the sliced almonds down the center, pressing them lightly to help adhere.

Bake the loaf until the top is browned, the edges begin to pull away from the pan, and a toothpick inserted in the center comes out clean, about 45 minutes (do not overbake), rotating the pan halfway through. Let the loaf cool in the pan for 8 minutes. Loosen the sides of the loaf and carefully turn it out (the pan will still be hot) onto the prepared rack and set right-side up.

To make the syrup: In a small saucepan over medium heat, combine the sugar, water, and salt and bring to a steamy simmer, constantly swirling the pan to dissolve the sugar, about 3 minutes. Continue simmering until glossy bubbles develop and the liquid is slightly thickened, about 3 minutes longer. Let the syrup cool to room temperature, add the vanilla and almond extract, and swirl to incorporate them.

While the loaf is still hot, use a long, thin skewer to poke deep holes (but don't go all the way through) on its bottom and sides, as well as along both sides of the almonds on top. Brush the syrup over the holes all over the loaf, working slowly to allow it to be absorbed. Return the loaf to the rack to cool to room temperature, if necessary. Slice and serve. Wrap in plastic wrap and store at room temperature for up to 2 days.

UNDERMOUNTAIN ALURLYATH

SERVES 2

One 1-pound English or standard cucumber, scrubbed but not peeled

2 ounces Amontillado sherry

1 ounce honey syrup

1 teaspoon fresh lemon juice

Small ice cubes

6 ounces plain seltzer, cold

COOK'S NOTE

Stirring in the cucumber juice, rather than shaking it with the other ingredients, prevents it from becoming too frothy.

Imported to the Rock of Bral by the barrel directly from the notorious dungeon called Undermountain, Undermountain Alurlyath is a sweet sherry wine made by desperate gnomish vintners that skulk about the mad vined halls of the dungeon. It is said that the grapes that grow in the labyrinth hold the secrets of the successful romance of flavors, and that a glass of genuine Undermountain Alurlyath, bursting with notes of honey and cucumber, will enchant its imbiber with the gift of supernatural confidence—a phenomenon known as the silver glow. Yet others hold the belief that this is, in fact, a fancy term for the growing false confidence that comes with drink.

Cut the cucumber in half crosswise, then cut two thin slices from the cut side of one half and reserve them for garnish. Chop the rest of the cucumber halves and transfer to a food processor. Process into a liquidy pulp, about 10 seconds, stopping once to scrape down the sides of the work bowl.

Line a medium bowl with a clean kitchen towel. Scrape the cucumber pulp into the center, gather the edges and corners of the towel, and, working over the bowl, squeeze and twist hard to wring out as much liquid as possible. Compost the pulp or reserve for another use.

Fill a cocktail shaker with the sherry, honey syrup, and lemon juice. Cover and shake to blend, about 10 seconds. Remove the cover, add 1 cup of the cucumber juice, and stir to combine.

Fill two rocks or wine glasses about halfway with ice, add half the sherry-cucumber mixture to each, top each with 3 ounces seltzer, and stir gently. Garnish each drink with a reserved cucumber slice before serving.

SOLAMNIA

Poisoned! Bri'An, Cleric of Tyr, sipped too deeply of
the quest item: a venomous wine! Now, our heroes
sail through Realmspace to KRYNN, the planet of the fabled
dragonlances, to seek a cure for Bri'An's deadly affliction!

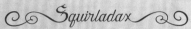

Squirladax

Emergency! Set we down on a—plain? Realm? I still do not understand this Wildspace we travel in, but I do understand brisk dispatch.

Bri'An, our most righteous cleric, has confessed to sipping the very QUEST ITEM, a wine called VENENO '18, revealed now to be a DEADLY POISON! Dint explains that, to save our comrade, we must make landfall immediately on a place called Krynn to seek out and seize vallenwood root. It is the only hope of restoration for our doomed Bri'An. Whilst Bri'An professes perfect, jovial health, Dint tells of painful gasping death should we choose to ignore this.

As this is how TPK starts, I will not have another on my conscience. We landed and set about our business immediately! Well—almost immediately. First, we should find something to eat. . . . Any adventure that begins on an empty stomach is doomed to fail!

Deelia

I tire of this quest! This spelljammer rattles me. All I wish is to serve the Raven Queen, and yet I have whispered no souls to find her embrace. All is gloom. This bright, green world of—what calls itself? Krynn? A city called Solanthus? The cheer of this place mocks my grim purpose: To bolster the Raven Queen's numbers in her everlasting battle with Orcus, Lord of the Damned and King of the Undead. Only then can I win her esteem, and perhaps then I might find a lasting peace in her Shadowfell.

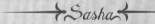

Sasha

Bri'An is the coolest cleric I have ever met. Not only does he effortlessly guzzle the local Tika's Honey Mead, not only can he tavern-brawl jerks with mighty punches, but he has also been helping me train as we both read from *Volo's Guide* on health and wisdom. It's the king's jewels, man!

But what I don't get: Why won't he cure himself of this nasty poison with his healing magic? He calls on Tyr with almost every step he takes . . . maybe it isn't working? I wish I was learnèd enough in such matters to help. Even now, Bri'An is rubbing Boar Hock Soup into my scalp to increase my cleverness, so recommends the guide.

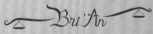

Bri'An

Why are the side-eyes spying me? What harm have Dragonmen done here on this Krynn, in this forsaken tavern called the Dog and Duck in the city of Solanthus? Tyr! Sasha and I beg forgiveness as we punch these jeering faces to weepiness. I shall sweep these sins off my plates and instead gorge myself of the delicious pastry-like Cloaks and seductive Tarsis-Style Shrimp so that I might have strength to serve your will. Praise be to Tyr!

Alas, I must have eaten too much Kendermore Cobbler—I feel not good.

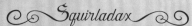 Squirladax

Huzzah! We have made the acquaintance of a local herbalist who tarries about the Vingaard River, yet he possesses no vallenwood root. Bri'An is now issuing a holy commandment that I share in some of his Salbread. Oh my! Tyr's heavens inside my mouth-hole!

I tell you, saucy reader, savor the small things. Especially when those small things can be crunched, swilled, or suckled. The life of many adventurers is fleeting, and they would do well to be mindful of the many curious places that their trail passes through. Any decrepit tavern could be home to a specialty that would be wondrous to any who had never tasted it before.

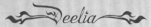 Deelia

I have gained two stone of regret and dread in this place, however, I cannot deny its Irlymeyer's Dragonfire Punch is supernatural. I am drunk and shall sleep a dead cold sleep.

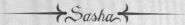 Sasha

Bri'An woke this morning, sweating, and coughing up black gunk. We're at this inn called the Black Tiger and I just talked to the inn keep. We gotta find this vallenwood root, but he warns that the mightiest and most mature vallenwood grows many leagues to the south in the lands of Abanasinia or something. Cool! Got it! Time to stretch my breath bellows to their limit and kick this side quest in the arse! Bri'An rocks and we got this!

 Bri'An

Tyr! My faith and health are tested! My throat fire burns icy, my scales dribble with unholy perspiration. Yet, I know I shall be healed by faith! Yea, even as this prayer leaves my lips, I feel vigor and not a small amount of vim returning. Yes recovery is upon me. What 'tis?! A roadside food stall serving yet more scrumptious morsels in this most delicious of realms?! This I must investigate!

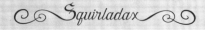 Squirladax

Bri'An is dead.

Boar Hock Soup

MAKES ABOUT 2½ QUARTS

2 pounds pork butt, or boneless country-style ribs, patted dry with a paper towel

Kosher salt and freshly ground black pepper

2 teaspoons extra-virgin olive oil

3 large carrots, peeled and chopped

2 medium yellow onions, chopped

2 large bay leaves

1 tablespoon minced fresh thyme

2 teaspoons ground fennel

1 tablespoon pressed or grated garlic

6 cups low-sodium chicken broth

1½ pounds Yukon gold or all-purpose potatoes, peeled and cut into ¾-inch chunks

1½ pounds leeks (white and light green parts), halved lengthwise and cut into ¾-inch pieces

1½ cups cooked, peeled chestnuts, coarsely chopped

1½ teaspoons sherry vinegar

½ cup chopped fresh parsley

Whether you make boar hock soup at the hearth of a cozy inn or on the campfire after the hunt, it is a meal unto itself. Like traditional bone-based soups, this version was originally created to let no part of a boar go wasted—in this case, the hock, or lower leg. But in times of plenty, you can still find soups filled with generous chunks of boar and without any bones to speak of. The genius of this recipe is in its recognition that boar is best complemented by a classic, creamy potato-leek soup. Brimming with whatever other veggies and spices you can get your hands on—even chestnuts are great in the mix—it is a savory, hearty celebration of the bounty of nature. Perfect for a cold, windy night.

Sprinkle the pork all over with 1½ teaspoons salt and ¾ teaspoon pepper.

In a large Dutch oven over medium heat, warm the olive oil until shimmering. Add the pork in a single layer and cook, undisturbed, until browned on the bottom, about 4 minutes. Turn the pork and continue cooking, undisturbed, to brown the second side, about 4 minutes longer. Transfer the pork to a large bowl, leaving the fat in the pot. When the pork is cool enough to handle, cut into ¾-inch pieces, discarding any large pieces of fat as you work. Set aside.

Return the Dutch oven to medium-high heat. Add the carrots, onions, bay leaves, thyme, fennel, and 1 teaspoon salt and cook, stirring and scraping the bottom of the pot with a wooden spoon to loosen and dissolve the caramelized bits, until the vegetables soften, about 5 minutes. Adjust the heat to medium-low, cover, and continue cooking, stirring occasionally, until the vegetables release their juices, about 6 minutes longer. Scrape the bottom of the pot to loosen and dissolve the caramelized bits. Adjust the heat to medium-high, add the garlic, and cook, stirring, until fragrant, about 40 seconds. Add the chicken broth and reserved pork with its accumulated juices and bring to a strong simmer. If foam forms on the surface, skim and discard it. Adjust the heat to low, cover, and let simmer until the pork is tender, about 40 minutes. CONTINUED ➤

BOAR HOCK SOUP CONTINUED

Adjust the heat to medium-high and bring the soup to a strong simmer. Add the potatoes, leeks, 1¼ cups of the chestnuts, 1 teaspoon salt, and 1 teaspoon pepper and return to a simmer, stirring. Adjust the heat to medium-low, replace the cover, and continue simmering until the potato cubes and leeks begin to soften, about 20 minutes longer. Remove the soup from the heat and let rest for about 30 minutes for the flavors to meld (the potatoes and leeks will finish cooking during the rest). Remove the bay leaves.

Transfer about ¾ cup of the soup, including some potato cubes, to a blender. Add the reserved ¼ cup chestnuts and blend as smooth as possible, about 30 seconds. Scrape the pureed mixture into the pot, add the vinegar, and stir to incorporate. If necessary, reheat the soup over medium heat, and taste and adjust the seasoning with additional salt and pepper, if necessary. Add most of the parsley, stir to blend, and sprinkle each portion with some of the remaining parsley before serving.

CLOAKS

MAKES ABOUT 20 CLOAKS

1½ pounds russet potatoes, peeled and cut into 1-inch chunks

5 tablespoons unsalted butter, cut into small cubes, at room temperature

1¼ cups half-and-half

Kosher salt and freshly ground black pepper

1 pinch freshly ground nutmeg

1 pinch cayenne pepper

1 egg plus 2 egg yolks, beaten

½ teaspoon baking powder

COOK'S NOTES

If you don't have a pastry bag, you can get away with a heavy-duty ziplock freezer bag as a substitute. Snip off about ⅜ inch from a bottom corner and fit the star tip into the hole, pushing it through from inside the bag.

Although you'll sacrifice the crisp ridges created by the star tip, you can use a spoon to shape the mounds into circles or ovals of about the same dimensions as the piped version, and run the tines of a fork over the surface to add texture.

Ideal as a filling comfort food, cloaks are finger snacks made from whipped potatoes, eggs, butter, and fresh spices. They get their name from their shape; as they bake, puffing into luxurious, golden-brown coverings, which look like warm winter cloaks. While some taverns pan-sear Cloaks in oil to give them a crispy, crunchy exterior, most establishments bake them and the dish is often thought to be best right out of the oven, soft and piping hot inside. On a cold day, a few Cloaks will warm you right up. In Kalaman they squeeze a bit of lemon juice on top to give it a little zing, and in springtime, it's not unusual to find a few edible flowers draped over them. Cloaks make a perfect side for fish or poultry, but eat enough of them, and you may end up skipping the main course entirely.

Place the potatoes in a large microwave-safe bowl, cover with a microwave-safe lid or plate, and microwave until very tender, about 18 minutes, stirring the potatoes twice during that time. Spread the potatoes on a baking sheet or large plate and let cool until you can handle them, about 5 minutes. Set a potato ricer over the empty bowl and rice the potatoes into it. Add half the butter cubes and stir to incorporate. Add the half-and-half, 2 teaspoons salt, ¾ teaspoon pepper, the nutmeg, and cayenne and stir to incorporate. Adjust the seasoning with additional salt and pepper, if necessary. Add the egg and yolks and baking powder and stir until the mixture is uniform and very smooth. Let cool to room temperature, add the remaining butter cubes, and fold to incorporate.

With a rack in the middle position, preheat the oven to 475°F. Line a baking sheet with parchment paper or a nonstick baking mat and coat it lightly with nonstick cooking spray.

Scrape the potato mixture into a piping bag fitted with a ½-inch star tip. Hold the filled pastry bag slightly above the prepared baking sheet and apply steady, gentle, downward pressure to pipe a mound roughly 2 inches in diameter and 2 inches high. Work your way out in a tight circular motion, and then back in again to build height. Pipe twenty mounds total, with about 1 inch between them (five rows of four mounds). Lightly coat the mounds with cooking spray.

Bake the cloaks until golden brown, about 14 minutes, rotating the baking sheet about halfway through. Let cool on the baking sheet for 2 minutes, then, using a spatula, transfer to a serving platter. Serve immediately.

SALBREAD

MAKES ONE 8-INCH
SQUARE LOAF

2 cups all-purpose flour

2 teaspoons baking powder

Kosher salt

1 cup granulated sugar

2 tablespoons finely grated lemon
zest or orange zest

1 cup plain yogurt
(preferably whole-milk)

2 eggs

½ teaspoon vanilla extract

½ cup neutral oil

COOK'S NOTE

*Salbread can be wrapped tightly
in plastic wrap and stored at room
temperature for up to 2 days.*

For those light-footed smallfolk who wander but still want to eat well, the kender of Kendermore look to salbread. This highly flavorful, square bread can last a full tenday in the pack before spoiling—or so it is said, as the actual expiration time frame has never been tested. These baked treats travel so well, they have found their way to many other corners of the multiverse and frequently show up in the packs of the halflings of Luiren, who are thought to be distant cousins of Krynn's kender. Usually made with lemon or orange peels and a touch of vanilla, these baked miracles not only taste delicious but also can prevent scurvy for those on ships or traveling in regions without access to fresh fruit.

With a rack in the middle position, preheat the oven to 350°F. Coat an 8-inch square pan with nonstick cooking spray and set aside.

In a medium bowl, combine the flour, baking powder, and ½ teaspoon salt and whisk to incorporate. In a large bowl, combine the sugar and lemon zest and stir until the sugar is moist and fragrant. Add the yogurt, eggs, vanilla, and neutral oil to the sugar and whisk vigorously to blend. Add the flour mixture and, using a flexible spatula, fold to blend the wet and dry ingredients just until no pockets of dry ingredients remain. Scrape the batter into the prepared pan and smooth the top.

Bake the loaf until lightly browned, a toothpick inserted in the center comes out clean, and the edges begin to pull away from the pan, about 40 minutes. Transfer the pan to a wire rack and let cool to room temperature, about 40 minutes. Turn the bread out of the pan and cut into squares to serve.

KENDER STUMBLENOODLES

SERVES 8

6 tablespoons unsalted butter, at room temperature

2 tablespoons all-purpose flour

1 tablespoon paprika

½ teaspoon garlic powder

1 pinch cayenne pepper

3 cups whole milk

2 teaspoons Dijon mustard

2 ounces cream cheese, cut into 4 pieces, at room temperature

Kosher salt and freshly ground black pepper

4½ cups lightly packed, coarsely grated sharp or extra-sharp Cheddar cheese (see Cook's Note)

12 ounces fusilli or rotini

1½ cups lightly packed, coarsely grated Gruyère cheese (see Cook's Note)

1⅓ cups panko breadcrumbs

COOK'S NOTES

It's best to grate your own cheese for this, as opposed to using pre-grated, which can be a touch grainy when melted because it includes additives to prevent clumping.

In this recipe, there's a lot of liquid and a lot of vigorous whisking, so choose a large, deep pot that can help contain the inevitable splashes.

Kender legends have a way of shifting and swaying merrily with the tides of the Blood Sea of Istar. An early tale held that kender stumblenoodles were born of a collision between two frantic kender cooks—when their pots mixed, it resulted in an unexpected alliance of flavors and ingredients. However, ask a kender adventurer, and you may as likely hear a yarn concerning a well-placed insult aimed toward a draconian corporal and his squad. As the bold kender scoundrel made haste to flee, he frantically threw about any valuables behind him to dissuade his pursuers. In his desperation, he ejected a small sack of mixed spices, hardened cheese, a jar of mustard, and several handfuls of uncooked spiral pasta shells that, as kender luck would have it, served as a meal of caltrops for draconian toes and sent the kender's pursuers stumbling into the mud. In honor of this brave kender's sacrifice (the loss of a perfectly good sack of pasta), kender across Krynn have memorialized the occasion in classic, good-humored kender fashion.

With a rack in the middle position, preheat the oven to 375°F. Smear a shallow 13 by 9-inch baking dish with 2 tablespoons of the butter, set it on a baking sheet, and set aside.

Fill a large pot with water, set over high heat, and bring to a boil.

Meanwhile, in another large pot over medium-high heat, melt 2 tablespoons butter. Whisk in the flour, paprika, garlic powder, and cayenne and cook, scraping the bottom of the pot, for 1 minute. Whisking constantly (and taking care to reach into the corners of the pot), gradually add the milk. Bring the mixture to a strong simmer, whisking the liquid and scraping the bottom of the pan often. Adjust the heat to medium and continue simmering and whisking until the sauce is thickened to the consistency of half-and-half, about 8 minutes longer.

Remove the pot from the heat; add the mustard, cream cheese, 1 teaspoon salt, and 1 teaspoon pepper; and whisk vigorously to melt and incorporate the cream cheese. Whisking constantly but gently, add the Cheddar, about 1 cup at a time, taking care to fully melt and incorporate each addition before adding the next. The sauce should be smooth and uniform.

Add 1 tablespoon salt and the fusilli to the pot of boiling water and cook, stirring occasionally to prevent sticking, according to the package directions until about 2 minutes short of al dente (there should be some resistance to the tooth). Drain the pasta, add it to the sauce, and stir to coat thoroughly. Let the mixture cool briefly, add the Gruyère, CONTINUED →

KENDER STUMBLENOODLES CONTINUED

and stir to incorporate. Adjust the seasoning with additional salt and pepper, if necessary. Scrape the mixture into the prepared baking dish and smooth into an even layer.

In a small microwave-safe bowl in the microwave oven, or in a small pot over medium heat, melt the remaining 2 tablespoons butter. Add the panko and ¼ teaspoon salt, season with pepper, and toss to coat the breadcrumbs. Sprinkle the panko evenly over the pasta.

Bake the pasta until heated through, the surface is browned, and the edges are bubbly, 30 to 40 minutes, rotating the pan halfway through. Let rest briefly, 8 to 10 minutes, before serving.

Tarsis-Style Shrimp

SERVES 4 TO 6

4 cups water

4 tablespoons fresh lemon juice, plus 2 teaspoons finely grated zest, and spent halves of the lemon reserved

¼ cup chopped fresh dill, stems reserved

Kosher salt

2 teaspoons whole black peppercorns

2 pounds extra-large shrimp, shelled and deveined

⅓ cup mayonnaise

¼ cup plain whole-milk Greek yogurt

6 scallions, white and green parts thinly sliced and kept separate

Freshly ground black pepper

1 large celery rib, trimmed and finely diced

A famous dish from the Inn of the Last Home, perhaps the most storied tavern in all of Krynn, Tarsis-Style Shrimp is a rich and creamy, belly-filling shellfish concoction. In this delectable maritime offering, poached shrimp are combined with a fresh yogurt-dill sauce, which can be delightful when dolloped atop long, homemade noodles. In a popular iteration of this dish, detailed in the culinary notes of Tika Waylan, former barmaid at the inn, "pulled turkey breast is substituted for the shrimp and enlivened with a dash of dry white wine." The sauce itself is so flavorful, it can perk up even the most mundane meats, something resourceful locals were forced to do post-Cataclysm, which left the Tarsis seaport landlocked. Regardless of your protein of choice, this is a not-to-be-missed regional delicacy.

In a large saucepan, combine the water, 3 tablespoons of the lemon juice, the spent lemon halves, dill stems, 1 teaspoon salt, the peppercorns, and shrimp. Set the pan over medium-high heat and cook, stirring occasionally, until the shrimp are pink, barely firm, and just cooked through, and the liquid temperature reaches 170°F on an instant-read thermometer, 10 to 15 minutes.

While the shrimp poach, set a colander in the sink, and fill a large bowl with ice water and set aside. Drain the poached shrimp in the colander, then, working quickly, transfer them to the ice water, leaving behind the lemon halves, dill stems, and peppercorns. Empty the colander, discarding its contents, and drain the shrimp again. Blot them dry with paper towels, and halve them lengthwise.

In a large bowl, combine the mayonnaise, yogurt, scallion whites, chopped dill, lemon zest, remaining 1 tablespoon lemon juice, ½ teaspoon salt, and ½ teaspoon pepper and whisk to incorporate. Add the shrimp and celery and fold to coat with the dressing. Cover and refrigerate so the flavors meld, about 2 hours.

Add most of the scallion greens to the shrimp and fold to combine. Adjust the seasoning with additional salt and pepper, if necessary. Sprinkle with the remaining scallion greens before serving.

The Inn...
the Last

Main Road, Last Hom

atter ....
rridge with fruits
d butterwhip ...
(by the loaf)
ad with seasonal toppin
Spiced Fried Potatoes'
t stuffed mushrooms and c
y dumplings (inquire)
de-me-overs'

PLATE OF SILVER

SERVES 4

1½ pounds small (2-inch) red-skinned or Yukon gold creamer potatoes, scrubbed

4 tablespoons extra-virgin olive oil

Kosher salt and freshly ground black pepper

About 2 ounces white anchovy fillets or boquerónes (see Cook's Note)

2 tablespoons chopped fresh parsley

COOK'S NOTES

Meaty marinated white anchovies are popular in Spain, where they're called boquerónes. *Instead of being packed in oil or salt, the anchovies are marinated in vinegar, which gives them a piquant flavor and whitens the flesh. They're less salty and intense than their tinned, oil-packed brethren.*

Using a second baking sheet will smash all the potatoes at once, whereas if you use the bottom of a mug or a potato masher, you will have to smash them individually.

In the Faerûnian land of Amn, there is a charming, well-appointed inn called Stargath House, which is known for a signature baked-potato-and-anchovy dish called the Plate of Silver. The meal is thusly named as consolation and warning to those who would sate their appetites by seeking the fabled treasures reputed to be hidden in an extensive network of booby-trapped and haunted cellars underneath the inn. The treasured gold is said to rattle inside the chest plates of helmed horrors that seek to claim the lives of trespassers. Many a guest has disobeyed the firm guidance of the courteous waitstaff and gone missing. It is tradition that when the unique delicacy is served, the staff and regulars of Stargath House rattle their gold coins inside tumblers as a way of presenting the recipient of Stargath hospitality with a choice: "Would you risk a cold and bitter death for the promise of haunted gold? Or would you kindly settle for a warm, tasty plate of silver, instead?" Both the dish and tradition have somehow found their way to Krynn, even though Stargath House is nowhere to be found on the planet.

With a rack in the middle position, preheat the oven to 450°F. Spread the potatoes on a baking sheet and roast until they are very tender, about 35 minutes. Remove the pan from the oven (leave the oven on) and set the potatoes aside to cool for about 10 minutes.

When the potatoes are cool enough to handle, transfer to a large bowl. Brush the same baking sheet with 2 tablespoons of the olive oil and sprinkle lightly with salt and pepper. Return the potatoes to the baking sheet, spaced about 2½ inches apart. With another baking sheet or the bottom of a mug or a potato masher, sharply press down on the potatoes to break their skins and compress the flesh until about ¾ inch thick. Brush the potatoes with the remaining 2 tablespoons olive oil and sprinkle lightly with salt and pepper. Return the potatoes to the oven and roast until deep golden brown, about 25 minutes longer, turning the baking sheet halfway through. Taste a small piece of a potato and adjust the seasoning with additional salt and pepper, if necessary.

Arrange the potatoes on a serving platter, lay an anchovy fillet over each one, and sprinkle with the parsley. Serve immediately.

STUFFED TROUT

SERVES 4

Four 10- to 12-ounce whole trout, gutted

2 teaspoons Old Bay seasoning

Freshly ground black pepper

2 large slices multigrain sandwich bread, crusts trimmed, torn into small pieces

3 tablespoons unsalted butter

Kosher salt

¼ cup minced shallot

¾ cup finely chopped red bell pepper

2 teaspoons pressed or grated garlic

2 teaspoons finely grated lemon zest, plus 1 tablespoon fresh lemon juice, plus lemon wedges for serving

⅓ cup chopped fresh parsley

COOK'S NOTE

Eating a whole trout is less intimidating than you may think. Peel back the skin to expose the flesh on one side. Starting at the equator of the exposed side of the fish, use a dinner knife to slide the flesh downward off the fish's skeleton. Repeat to slide off the flesh above the equator. Flip the fish and repeat to release the flesh on the second side.

Those who happen upon the Solamnian city of Palanthus would be fools not to drop by the A Taste of Silvanost restaurant and try its famous Stuffed Trout. Of course, what the trout is stuffed with is anyone's guess. According to the menu (which is written in Silvanesti), you'll find "specially prepared mixtures" inside. But rumor has it the stuffing is composed of breadcrumbs made from the fresh-baked loaves of the elven proprietor Solamna Farseer, and seasoned with a rare spice known as Old Bay, named for the Bay of Branchala, next to which the city rests.

With a rack in the middle position, preheat the oven to 450°F. Line a rimmed baking sheet with parchment paper or a nonstick baking mat and set aside.

Rinse each trout under cold running water and, using a paper towel, dry very well, inside and out. Sprinkle the cavity of each trout evenly with ½ teaspoon Old Bay and ¼ teaspoon black pepper.

In a food processor, pulse the bread into crumbs the size of grains of rice, about five 2-second pulses.

In a medium skillet over medium heat, melt 2 tablespoons of the butter. Add the breadcrumbs and ½ teaspoon salt and season with pepper. Cook, stirring constantly, until deeply browned and crisp, about 6 minutes. Scrape the toasted breadcrumbs into a medium bowl and set aside.

Wipe the skillet clean and return it to medium heat. Add the remaining 1 tablespoon butter and let warm until melted. Add the shallot, bell pepper, and ½ teaspoon salt and cook, stirring constantly, until the vegetables start to soften, about 2 minutes. Adjust the heat to low, cover, and cook until the vegetables appear moist, about 1½ minutes longer. Add the garlic and lemon zest and cook, stirring, until fragrant, about 40 seconds. Scrape the mixture into the bowl with the toasted breadcrumbs, add the lemon juice and parsley, and stir to combine into a stuffing. Adjust the seasoning with additional salt and pepper, if necessary.

Place the trout on the prepared baking sheet. Spoon about ⅓ cup of the stuffing into the cavity of each trout, pressing it in with your fingers. Arrange the fish so there is about 1 inch between them.

Bake the trout until they feel firm when pressed gently with your finger, and the thickest part of the fish registers 140°F on an instant-read thermometer, about 12 minutes. Let the trout rest for 5 minutes. Using a fish spatula or another long spatula, carefully transfer the trout to a serving platter and serve with lemon wedges.

KENDER LOAF

SERVES 6 TO 8

One 1-pound loaf French or Italian bread (see Cook's Note)

⅓ cup granulated sugar

2 teaspoons finely grated lemon or orange zest

⅓ cup light brown sugar

1 teaspoon ground cinnamon

1¾ cups half-and-half

2 eggs plus 2 egg yolks

1 teaspoon vanilla extract

Kosher salt

1 cup golden raisins

5 tablespoons unsalted butter, at room temperature

COOK'S NOTES

The best bread for this recipe is a round or oval loaf with a thin, light-colored crust. Avoid artisan or sourdough loaves with thick crusts. If you accidentally break through the bottom of the loaf while removing the crumb, patch the hole with a crusty piece from the top.

Like any bread pudding, a scoop of ice cream, a dollop of whipped cream, or a drizzle of custard sauce are welcome partners.

Leftover slices of the pudding are great for hearty French toast!

Kender loaf, or raston pastry as it has been called, is a filling, raisin-specked dessert to round out a hearty meal. However, in its earlier incarnations, raston pastry dated back to the first Dragon War, when not even scraps of stale bread could be discarded. Crusts of stale bread were habitually tossed into a basin and later mashed to create livestock feed, but the kender saw an opportunity. Stale bread was separated from other half-finished morsels; soaked in water; sugared, spiced, and dried; then served up as what was known as kender loaf, the pre-owned bread. So popular was kender loaf that the process was refined with eggs, cream, and spices, evolving into the bread puddings we know today.

With a rack in the middle position, preheat the oven to 350°F.

With the loaf right-side up, use a serrated knife to cut around the perimeter of the bread, about 1 inch from the sides, taking care to not pierce the bottom. Pull off the top of the bread and tear it into roughly 1-inch pieces. Hollow out the rest of the loaf by carefully tearing out the crumb in roughly 1-inch pieces. Set the bread shell aside and spread the torn pieces on a rimmed baking sheet. Bake the bread pieces, tossing occasionally, until toasted and light golden, 20 to 25 minutes, rotating the baking sheet about halfway through. Remove from the oven and let cool to room temperature, about 10 minutes. Leave the oven on.

Meanwhile, in a large bowl, combine the granulated sugar and lemon zest and stir until moist and fragrant. In a small bowl, combine 1 tablespoon of the lemon sugar, the brown sugar, and cinnamon, breaking up any lumps of brown sugar with your fingers, and set aside. In the large bowl with the lemon sugar, whisk in the half-and-half, eggs and egg yolks, vanilla, and 1 pinch salt and continue whisking until well blended. Add the toasted bread and raisins, then press and stir to submerge them as much as possible. Set aside to soak until the bread is thoroughly saturated, stirring and resubmerging occasionally, about 20 minutes.

Spread 3 tablespoons of the butter on the inside of the bread shell, then sprinkle with half of the brown sugar mixture. Place the bread shell on a rimmed baking sheet and fill with the soaked bread mixture, gently mounding it. Sprinkle the remaining brown sugar mixture over the surface of the filling and dot with the remaining 2 tablespoons butter.

Bake the pudding until a toothpick or thin knife inserted into the center comes out clean, 35 to 40 minutes, rotating the baking sheet about halfway through. Set the pudding on a wire rack and let cool until just warm or at room temperature. Using a serrated knife, slice the pudding and serve.

KENDERMORE COBBLER

SERVES 4 TO 6

FILLING

3 pounds firm but ripe peaches, peeled, pitted, and cut into 1½-inch wedges, or 8 cups frozen peaches, thawed

3 tablespoons granulated sugar

1 pinch kosher salt

3 tablespoons light brown sugar

1 tablespoon cornstarch

¼ teaspoon ground cloves

3 tablespoons bourbon, amber or dark rum, brandy, or cognac (see Cook's Note)

1 teaspoon vanilla extract

1 cup fresh or frozen blueberries (see Cook's Note)

TOPPING

5 tablespoons granulated sugar

¼ teaspoon ground cinnamon

1½ cups all-purpose flour

1½ teaspoons baking powder

½ teaspoon kosher salt

1 egg

⅓ cup buttermilk

3 tablespoons unsalted butter, melted and cooled

1 teaspoon vanilla extract

COOK'S NOTES

You can substitute 3 tablespoons of the exuded peach juices for the booze, if you wish.

If you use frozen blueberries, don't worry about defrosting them.

Nothing warms the soul quite like the scent of a freshly baked kender cobbler. The flavor of this effervescent blend of peaches, dark berries, vanilla, cloves, and liquor (for the brave, a sizable enough dash to make your toes tingle) is as fascinating as the diminutive folk who invented it. Kender—said to be birthed of magic and chaos—approach food in much the same manner as they traverse the worlds of the multiverse: adventurously. The buttery, flaky topping oozing with soft, chopped peaches should be enough, but when combined with blueberries, the cobbler filling brightens in a curiously kender way. This dessert is especially popular on Mid-year Day in Sixthmonth, which also happens to be Peach Month in Ansalon, but it remains the dessert of choice for the kender of Krynn regardless of holiday or season. Often served as a cobbler, sometimes as a crumble, but *never* to be skipped, especially when offered warm with a hefty dollop of fresh whipped cream.

To make the filling: In a large strainer set over a large bowl, toss the peaches, granulated sugar, and salt and set aside to drain for 1 hour, tossing them once or twice during that time. Pour off the accumulated peach juices and reserve for another use, if desired.

In a small bowl, combine the brown sugar, cornstarch, cloves, bourbon, and vanilla and whisk to incorporate.

Add the blueberries to the peaches, then add the cornstarch mixture and toss to coat. Scrape the filling into an 8-inch square pan with 2-inch sides, and spread into an even layer. Set aside.

With a rack in the middle position, preheat the oven to 425°F. Line a baking sheet with parchment paper or a nonstick baking mat and set aside. Butter the inside of a ¼ cup dry measuring cup.

To make the topping: In a small bowl, combine 2 teaspoons of the granulated sugar and the cinnamon and stir to incorporate, then set aside.

In a large bowl, combine the flour, baking powder, salt, and remaining 4 tablespoons plus 1 teaspoon granulated sugar and whisk to incorporate. In a medium bowl, combine the egg, buttermilk, melted butter, and vanilla and whisk until uniform. Add the buttermilk mixture to the flour mixture and, using a large spoon, fold and stir until a dough forms and no dry patches remain (do not overmix).

Add enough of the dough to fill three-fourths of the prepared measuring cup and lightly pat into the cup to shape it. Turn out the dough onto the prepared baking sheet. Repeat with the remaining dough for a total of nine rounds, spacing them 1 inch apart. Sprinkle with the reserved cinnamon sugar.

Bake the rounds until puffed, very lightly browned on the bottom, and partially cooked through, about 7 minutes, rotating the baking sheet halfway through. Transfer the parbaked biscuits to a plate and set aside.

Set the pan with the filling on the baking sheet. Bake until the peaches begin to soften and release their juices, 30 to 40 minutes. Arrange the parbaked biscuits over the peaches and continue baking until the peaches are tender and the biscuits are golden brown, about 15 minutes longer. Let cool on a wire rack for 25 minutes. Serve warm or at room temperature.

IRLYMEYER'S DRAGONFIRE PUNCH

MAKES ABOUT 2½ QUARTS

3 cups cranberry juice cocktail

⅓ cup frozen orange juice concentrate, thawed

½ cup frozen pineapple juice concentrate, thawed

3 tablespoons fresh lemon juice

1 cup brandy

1 cup large ice cubes (see Cook's Note), plus more for serving

One 750 ml bottle Prosecco or other sparkling wine, cold

1 large orange, scrubbed and thinly sliced

COOK'S NOTE

A small block of ice will melt more slowly than the cup of ice cubes. To make such a block, fill a 1-quart plastic container (such as a deli container) with water and freeze it overnight. To loosen the block of ice from the container, hold it briefly under hot running water.

The golden rule with any good tavern punch is that, when going down, it should feel like you were struck by a physical one and make you more inclined to throw one. Such is the case with the potent potable sometimes called Irlymeyer's Dragonfire Punch. A creation of the mysterious mixologist for whom the drink is named, and perfected by Otik Sandath of the Inn of the Last Home, this refreshing beverage is chock-full of domestic and imported juices from across Krynn, including cranberry, orange, and pineapple. The "punch" comes from the generous amounts of brandy and sparkling wine. Originally named for its use of poisonous dragon's rose blossoms, the recipe has changed significantly over the years, but its effect upon patrons has not.

In a large bowl or pitcher, combine the cranberry juice cocktail, orange juice concentrate, pineapple juice concentrate, lemon juice, and brandy and stir to blend. (This mix can be made 1 day ahead, covered, and refrigerated.)

When ready to serve, add the ice to the mix and stir to chill and blend. Add the Prosecco and stir gently. Fill each glass with ice, pour in the punch, and garnish with an orange slice.

TIKA'S HONEY MEAD

SERVES 2

Small ice cubes for shaking

4 ounces off-dry (almost dry), traditional-style mead (such as Oliver Winery and Vineyards Camelot Mead)

2 ounces fresh orange juice

1½ ounces gin (such as London dry)

1 ounce honey syrup

½ ounce fresh lemon juice

2 orange twists

To chill a cocktail glass or coupe, put it in the freezer for an hour before using.

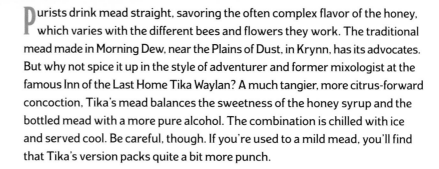

Purists drink mead straight, savoring the often complex flavor of the honey, which varies with the different bees and flowers they work. The traditional mead made in Morning Dew, near the Plains of Dust, in Krynn, has its advocates. But why not spice it up in the style of adventurer and former mixologist at the famous Inn of the Last Home Tika Waylan? A much tangier, more citrus-forward concoction, Tika's mead balances the sweetness of the honey syrup and the bottled mead with a more pure alcohol. The combination is chilled with ice and served cool. Be careful, though. If you're used to a mild mead, you'll find that Tika's version packs quite a bit more punch.

Chill two coupes or cocktail glasses (see Cook's Note).

Fill a large cocktail shaker about halfway with ice and add the mead, orange juice, gin, honey syrup, and lemon juice. Cover and shake until blended and chilled, about 30 seconds. Strain the mixture into the chilled glasses. Run an orange twist around the rim of each glass and then drop it in before serving.

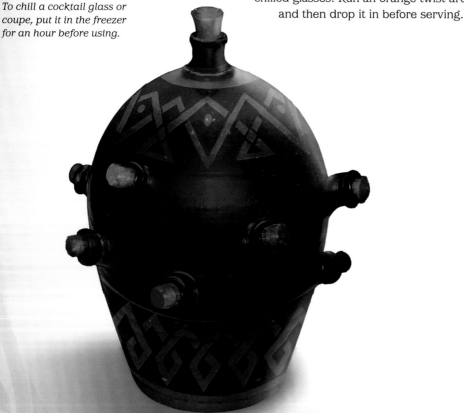

LOST IN REALMSPACE

Mourning the tragic loss of their
comrade, our hungry heroes drift
aimlessly in REALMSPACE!

Squirladax

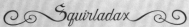

Another fallen comrade, another Total Planning Katastrophe, and only myself to blame. The dagger of fate indeed cuts deep. Whilst our time with Bri'An was short, somehow his death stings most profoundly.

He was a dragon among men, a man among dragons. I pray he restèth in the house of Tyr, but my bitter goblin intuition tells me otherwise. I commit a portion of this Ruby Cordial (not to be confusèd with Ruby) to the Astral Sea in your honor, and now I sip its cherried juices.

Meanstwhile, the bronze-armored little man called Dint has set us sail to places unknown. Whatmatter. I again lead the Bureau toward certain death and without a healer no less. I am no leader. A poet, surely, but a leader? My plans know only failure. Only the promised glint of Astral Diamonds keepeth me going. Oh, how I long to return to my homeland, the soothing Caves of Calmness, with sweet Ruby and to hang up my adventuring leathers for good.

Sasha

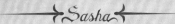

I don't understand it. *Volo's Guide to Bodily Health* says that Bri'An's symptoms were those of sour health and worsening humors. I did what it said and applied last-minute leeches to administer a bloodletting, and even screamed at the leeches to suck faster! But you could see on their tired, defeated little faces that they couldn't drain away the poison fast enough to save him! They were too late. I was too late. . . . I'm always too late. Not fast enough, not strong enough.

Oh, that I could smite the poison, smash it, but I am no more a healer than I am a fighter. I'm sorry, honest and faithful Bri'An. You deserved better and we failed you.

I now must eat the saltiest of Breaded Bird Cutlets and Beluir Poached Salmon that Dint keeps aboard to replenish the salts that have leaked from my eyes.

I will never be a real fighter.

Deelia

I am troubled this day. What if Squirladax is right and there's nothing after death?

No. No, it cannot be. Even now, the Raven Queen awaits me in the Shadowfell, pleased with her newest prize: the fresh soul of a dragonborn cleric delivered upon the raven I sent from Krynn. Or I thought I spied a nearby raven, did I not?! Even as I whispered to Bri'An the words I learned from the Lords of Shadow's Edge . . . ?

Shadow's Edge.

I have a confession to make, cursed reader. For I was cast out and banished from the Shadow's Edge Academy. I know that death **will** come for me; for I know that great spell powers and other adventuring grits are beyond my prowess for only I know that I am a Shadow's Edge drop-out.

It's not all for my fault. BETRAYED I was, and by my good friend, and fellow, if jealous, student!

And so too are you, Bri'An, betrayed . . . by my incompetence. What betrayals did you hide, Bri'An?

Before we committed his soulless corpse to the fertile grounds of Solamnia, we performed the rite of Journey's End—that is, we cleared it of all effects. Curiously, upon his scaled figure he carried a modest, but not insubstantial cache of wealth: rings of gold, a jeweled medallion, and trinkets of silver. He even carried blades. I've never known a cleric to carry such items. But no matter. Bri'An was jolly. Bri'An was good . . . if Bri'An was even his real name.

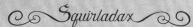

Squirladax

We've now been hours in this sea of astralness, but my spirits have begun to lighten (as has my head due to the copious amounts of Ruby Cordial).

The bronze-plate-hidden gnome called Dint has advised that we, the "Quaternate Tetrad," are to be the guests of honor at a grand feast at a luxurious castle called Ravenloft, where we are to deliver the wine, Veneno '18. Finally, the end of a successful quest! I know not this Ravenloft, but it sounds lofty and prestigious.

Dint has already shown us a most florid invitation, written in practiced calligraphy, which bodes that this may be the most extraordinary meal of our lives, with a dessert of FIVE ASTRAL DIAMONDS! If only . . . if only there were more of us to enjoy it.

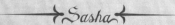

Dint

I must improve the disposition and torso shape of these humanoids with an excessive meal. Their figures musssst be modmodified ffffor maximum nnnnnutrient density. Once dispatched to RRRRR-Ravenloft, I shall run a diagnostic as I appear appear to be malfunctioning.

Sasha

Dint cooks?! The deck of the Dashor was splayed with an endless and delightful repast of morsels that threatened to burst my goblin tum! It was a bloodthemed meal, I must guess, in honor of the blood shed by dear Bri'An—a memorial supper. Oh, the flavors! The Blood of Vol was a fireball of flavors as was a dish called Thrakel-Seared Beef in Red Sauce. This runny red meal paired perfectly with more Ruby Cordial. We engorged and imbibed, welcoming with open arms the food-and-booze-induced coma that was fated us.

Sasha

That dinner was freaking insane. I can barely move. Even my leeches are fat. I am worried about Dint, though. Did he always have a limp? And fall down a lot? And nap in the middle of sentences?

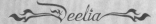

Dint

Approaccccching Barovia. AUTOGNOME syssystems mmmmalfunctioning. M-m-m-must replenish p-p-power source. Jewel of Javanium exhausted. . . . ppoowwerrrr doooowwwwnn. . . .

Deelia

Umm. . . . Dint has fallen to clackety limpness and we seem to be speeding and spiraling through a thick mist. Does anyone know how to fly this thing?

Beluir Poached Salmon

MAKES ABOUT 2 CUPS

8 ounces salmon fillet, skin left on and any pinbones removed

8 ounces cream cheese, at room temperature

1½ tablespoons fresh lemon juice, plus more as needed

½ teaspoon paprika

1 pinch cayenne pepper

Kosher salt and freshly ground black pepper

6 tablespoons minced shallots

3 ounces cold-smoked Nova Scotia–style salmon, finely chopped

¼ cup minced fresh chives

Crostini or thinly sliced baguette for serving

Capers for serving (see Cook's Note)

COOK'S NOTES

If you'd like to dampen the capers' saltiness, rinse them under cold running water and blot dry before serving.

The salmon can be refrigerated in an airtight container for up to 2 days.

Known as the unofficial capital of the former halfling nation of Luiren, Beluir was well regarded for its friendly folk, its strategic port location, and, of course, its food. The city's proximity to forests, rich farmland, and the sea made it an obvious destination for chefs and diners from across the Realms. And few dishes stood out more than Beluir's famous poached salmon. Available at virtually any eating house in town, the most traditional preparation came from the Friendly Burrow tavern, which created a mouthwatering spread, comprising both fresh and smoked salmon, herbs, cream cheese, and a touch of cayenne, served atop a baguette with a sprinkle of capers. If you couldn't get into the Friendly Burrow (it was always packed), the Cold Duck Inn made a worthy representation, and they even had rooms for rent that could accommodate "tall folk" guests who needed a rest after all that dining. While Luiren is no more, this famous dish can still be found on board various halfling-crewed spelljammers who commandeered this dish as their own.

Fill a wide pot with about 3 inches of water, set a steamer basket into the pot (the water should not touch the steamer), cover, and bring to a boil over high heat. Add the salmon fillet, skin-side down, cover, and steam until just slightly translucent at the center, 6 to 9 minutes, depending on its thickness (the salmon will finish cooking as it cools). Transfer the salmon to a plate and set aside to cool to room temperature. When ready to handle, remove and discard the skin and break the flesh into large flakes.

In a food processor, combine the cream cheese, lemon juice, paprika, cayenne, and ½ teaspoon salt and season with black pepper. Process until smooth, stopping to scrape down the sides of the work bowl, using a flexible spatula as necessary. Add about half the steamed salmon and process until well combined, again stopping to scrape down the sides of the work bowl as necessary. Scrape the mixture into a medium bowl, add the remaining steamed salmon, the shallots, smoked salmon, and chives. Using the spatula, fold the mixture until well combined. Adjust the seasoning with additional lemon juice, salt, and pepper, if necessary. Cover and refrigerate to let the flavors blend, about 30 minutes.

When ready to serve, let rest at room temperature for a few minutes so it loses its chill, then pass crostini and capers alongside.

BLACK LOTUS ROOT

SERVES 6 AS A SNACK

12 ounces fresh lotus root, peeled and sliced ¼ inch thick

Kosher salt

⅔ cup unseasoned rice vinegar

⅔ cup water

3 tablespoons plus 1 teaspoon granulated sugar

1½ tablespoons butterfly pea powder (see Cook's Note)

1 medium shallot, very thinly sliced

COOK'S NOTE

Butterfly pea powder is made from the butterfly pea plant and is available online and at some natural food stores with a good selection of herbs and spices. In combination with an acidic ingredient, such as the rice vinegar, it produces a vivid purple tint.

There is one curriculum rarely discussed at Strixhaven University—feasting. But with offerings at the school's refectories as eclectic as its student body, aspiring mages from across the multiverse are exposed to exotic, colorful, and delicious meals to keep their learning minds inspired. At the Bow's End Tavern, a popular campus eatery, one culinary rite of passage is the pickled Black Lotus Root. This earthy yet tangy treat is an addictive nibble, notorious for turning the tongues of those who eat it purple. First years often flash their lilac tongues on campus like a badge of courage. Notably, Black Lotus Root pairs well with nearly any of the colorful (and alchemical) concoctions on tap.

In a large bowl, soak the sliced lotus in water to cover for about 15 minutes. Drain the lotus and set aside. Refill the bowl with ice water.

Meanwhile, fill a medium saucepan with water and bring to a boil over high heat. Add ½ teaspoon salt and the lotus, cover, and cook until just tender-crisp, about 1½ minutes (the water won't return to a full boil). Drain the lotus and immediately add to the ice water to stop the cooking. Drain again and set aside.

Set the saucepan over medium-high heat; add the vinegar, ⅔ cup water, and sugar; and bring to a bare simmer, whisking to dissolve the sugar. Remove from the heat, add the butterfly pea powder and ¼ teaspoon salt, and whisk to combine, taking care to break up any small clumps of powder. Add the blanched lotus and the shallot, submerging them in the liquid as much as possible, and set aside to cool to room temperature, about 30 minutes.

Transfer the contents of the saucepan to a container, taking care to submerge the lotus as much as possible. Cover and refrigerate until the lotus is a deep shade of purple, at least 24 hours or up to 5 days. Serve cold.

Green Dragon Blackbread Muffins

MAKES 12 MUFFINS

1 cup all-purpose flour

½ cup dark rye flour

½ cup medium-grind cornmeal (preferably stone-ground)

2 teaspoons unsweetened cocoa powder (preferably Dutch-process)

1½ teaspoons baking soda

¾ teaspoon kosher salt

½ teaspoon baking powder

¼ cup neutral oil

4 tablespoons unsalted butter, melted and cooled, plus butter at room temperature for serving

⅓ cup unsulfured molasses (not blackstrap)

¼ cup packed dark brown sugar

1 egg

¾ cup buttermilk

¾ cup currants or raisins (optional)

COOK'S NOTES

Choose a nonstick muffin tin with a gold-tone, or medium-grey finish (or other medium tone). These produce nicely browned baked goods, neither too dark (as is often the case with heavily sweetened batters in very dark bakeware), nor too light.

Baking soda, the primary leavener here, starts to react with the acidic ingredients in the batter on contact. Work quickly to fill the muffin tin, and get it into the oven at once so you don't lose too much leavening oomph.

Blackbread is a palm-size circular loaf of pumpernickel that demands to be served warm and topped with sweet butter. A base of stone-ground cornmeal, dark rye flour, and a dash of unsweetened cocoa bolster the dark colors and texture. Buttermilk, molasses, and dark brown sugar round out this versatile bread with an almost honeyed nuance, which dips nicely in surplus gravy. You aren't doing it right unless a sizable slab of salted yak butter or the like is slathered on top to melt into its deep, dark nooks. A fancier version, usually served as a meal in itself, has currants or dried fruits rolled in, providing an even chewier and heartier experience. Blackbread is often sold in loaves by the bunch, but they are equally delectable in a portable muffin form, as they are served at the Green Dragon Inn in the Free City of Greyhawk. Blackbread's versatility makes it a great day starter reheated in a skillet, with—you guessed it—additional butter glistening atop. A notable version of this exists in loaf form in Saltmarsh and its nautical outskirts. In truth, whether eaten from a loaf or as a muffin, it's a classic and frugal dark bread that finds its way into many a larder.

With a rack in the middle position, preheat the oven to 400°F. Coat a 12-cup muffin tin with nonstick cooking spray, or line with paper liners, and set aside.

In a large bowl, combine both flours, the cornmeal, cocoa powder, baking soda, salt, and baking powder and whisk to incorporate. In a medium bowl, combine the neutral oil, melted butter, molasses, and brown sugar and whisk, to break up any sugar lumps, until uniform. Add the egg and buttermilk and whisk until uniform. Add the wet mixture to the dry mixture and, using a flexible spatula, fold until they're incorporated into a batter with no dry patches (do not overmix). Fold in the currants (if using). Working quickly, using a large spoon or portion scoop, evenly divide the batter among the prepared muffin cups.

Bake the muffins until a toothpick inserted in the center of one or two comes out clean, about 15 minutes, rotating the muffin tin halfway through (do not overbake). Let the muffins cool in the tin for about 12 minutes, then remove to a wire rack to cool further, if desired. Serve with room-temperature butter.

The Green Dragon Inn

River Quarter · Free City of Greybank

Food

Eggs, boiled and ...
Sausage/Bumble...
"Orc" Bacon - the...
Muffins with berries (three slices) .... 2 sp
Honey butter .... 5 sp
Smoked Okerlund beer Wheel ....
Perrelandy Green .... 3 sp
Nutbread loaf .... 3 sp
Fried bread and spices .... 7 sp
Greens with garlic .... 5 sp
Soup, leek and boar .... 1 sp
Fried mushroom in garlic sauce .... 2 sp
Wolf's Plate (sausage and potatoes) .... 5 sp
... ragout (turnips and onions) ....

Mutton meatloaf ....
Wolf steak ....
Venison, marinated in red wine and spices .... 7 sp
Broiled cruytfish in butter and scallions ....
Spit roast stuffed goose .... 1 sp
Pleasures of the deep in hot broth and sherry .... 1 sp
Barter Freaks Surrogate Steaks .... 1 sp
Heroes' Feast (only available Fridays when cleric is present) .... 10 sp
D'emberville onion soup .... 1 sp
The Endless Platter - river eels, smoked, all you can eat .... 60 sp
Bread pudding, warm, with milk and butter .... 5 sp
Berry tart .... 3 sp
Mincemeat story .... 3 sp
Ice cake .... 2 sp
Gingerbread man "Greybank style" ....

Drinks

Served by the pint unless it says otherwise

.... 2 sp
.... 1 sp Velunto Firewater Wine
.... 1 sp Mulled wine
Brandy, local (gill)
Kentish Brandy, imported (gill)
Heart Brandy, special (gill)
Wild Elixir liquers (gill)
Purple fireymaid's ...
Mashed tea ...
.... 1 sp

THRAKEL-SEARED BEEF IN RED SAUCE

SERVES 4

1 pound flank steak, trimmed of fat

2 tablespoons Shaoxing rice wine or dry sherry

1 tablespoon soy sauce

2½ teaspoons cornstarch

½ teaspoon granulated sugar

2 tablespoons low-sodium chicken broth or water

2 teaspoons unseasoned rice vinegar

2 teaspoons toasted sesame oil

3 tablespoons ketchup

Kosher salt and freshly ground black pepper

1 tablespoon grated fresh ginger

1 tablespoon pressed or grated garlic

6 scallions, trimmed, white parts minced and green parts cut into ½-inch pieces

3 tablespoons neutral oil

1 pound plum tomatoes, cored, halved lengthwise, seeded, and halves cut lengthwise into thirds (see Cook's Note)

1 medium yellow onion, halved from pole to pole and sliced lengthwise

COOK'S NOTES

You can substitute one 14½-ounce can diced tomatoes, drained, for the plum tomatoes, and use 2 tablespoons of their liquid instead of the broth.

Serve this with hot freshly cooked rice—brown or white.

Despite its reputation as a puritanical theocracy, Eberron's central Khorvaire nation of Thrane has a long and storied culinary tradition. Their culinary mastery is on no greater display than during the Feast of the Silver Flame, where one dish stands above the rest: Thrakel-Seared Beef in Red Sauce. True to Thranish tradition, strips of flank steak are drowned in a tomato-based sauce with hints of ginger, soy, and garlic. Scallions and onions add some kick in this explosion of flavor renowned through Eberron.

Cut the flank steak against the grain into ½-inch-thick slices, each strip cut crosswise into thirds.

In a medium bowl, combine 1 tablespoon of the rice wine, the soy sauce, 2 teaspoons of the cornstarch, and the sugar and whisk to blend. Add the beef, stir to coat, and let rest at room temperature for 15 to 30 minutes. Meanwhile, in a small bowl, combine the remaining 1 tablespoon rice wine, remaining ½ teaspoon cornstarch, the chicken broth, rice vinegar, and sesame oil and stir to blend. Add the ketchup, 1 teaspoon salt, and 1 teaspoon pepper; mix until well blended; and set aside. In another small bowl, combine the ginger, garlic, scallion whites, and 2 teaspoons of the neutral oil; stir to mix; and set aside.

In a large nonstick skillet over high heat, warm 1 tablespoon of the neutral oil until shimmering. Swirl the skillet to coat the bottom with oil, add half the beef in a single layer and cook, undisturbed, until browned on the bottom, about 1 minute. Flip the beef, continue to cook, stirring occasionally, until brown on both sides, about 1 minute longer. Transfer to a large bowl, and set aside. Add another 1 tablespoon neutral oil to the skillet and repeat to cook the remaining beef. Transfer to the bowl.

Adjust the heat to medium-high, add the remaining 1 teaspoon of neutral oil to the skillet, and warm until shimmering. Swirl the skillet to coat the bottom with oil, add the tomatoes, toss to coat, and arrange in a single layer. Cook, undisturbed, until browned on the bottom, about 3 minutes. Transfer half the tomatoes to the bowl with the beef. Add the onion to the skillet and cook, stirring occasionally, for about 1½ minutes. Add the scallion greens and cook, stirring occasionally, until they start to wilt, about 1½ minutes longer. Adjust the heat to medium, clear the center of the pan, add the ginger-garlic mixture, and cook, stirring and mashing, until fragrant, about 45 seconds. Whisk the ketchup mixture to recombine, add to the skillet, and cook, stirring constantly until thickened, about 45 seconds. Return the beef and cooked tomatoes to the pan and cook, stirring constantly, until heated through and coated with sauce, about 1 minute longer. Serve immediately.

ORNABRA

SERVES 6

8 medium carrots, peeled

3½ pounds boneless lamb shoulder roast (see Cook's Note), trimmed of excess fat and cut into 1½-inch chunks

Kosher salt and freshly ground black pepper

2 tablespoons all-purpose flour

About 1½ tablespoons neutral oil

2 large onions, chopped

3 bay leaves

1 tablespoon minced fresh rosemary or thyme, or a combination

1 tablespoon tomato paste

2 cups low-sodium chicken broth

2 pounds Yukon gold potatoes, peeled and cut into ¾-inch pieces

1 teaspoon cider vinegar

½ cup chopped fresh parsley

Ornabra is a hearty meal and something of a badge of honor for those who have eaten it. This dish has been served for many generations by the hard-working denizens of Purskul (the "Granary City"), a bustling and notable caravan stop inland from Athkatla, between Amn's Cloud Peak and the Small Teeth mountains in West Faerûn. Lamb and potato stew is simmered for hours, then drained before being wrapped in thick and chewy flatbread the size of a small shield. As popular with Purskul's human constituents as with its sizable half-orc population, this street food is enough to fill a humanoid belly for two meals and is commonly scooped up by on-the-go, coin-conscious caravanners along the Southern Trade Way.

With a rack in the lower-middle position, preheat the oven to 325°F.

Finely chop two of the carrots and set aside. Cut the remaining six carrots into 1-inch chunks and set aside separately.

In a medium bowl, toss the lamb with 1½ teaspoons salt, 1 teaspoon pepper, and the flour to coat.

In a large, ovenproof sauté pan or Dutch oven over medium-high heat, warm 2 teaspoons of the neutral oil until shimmering. Add a third of the lamb (the pieces should be close together in a single layer, but not touching; do not crowd the pan) and cook, undisturbed, until deeply browned on the bottom, about 3½ minutes. Flip the pieces and cook, undisturbed, until the second side is deeply browned, about 3½ minutes longer. Transfer the lamb to a large bowl. Repeat to brown the remaining lamb in another one or two batches (warming more neutral oil for each batch and adjusting the heat as necessary to avoid scorching).

Spoon off all but 1 tablespoon of fat. Set the pan over medium heat, add the finely chopped carrots, onions, bay leaves, rosemary, and ½ teaspoon salt and cook, occasionally stirring and scraping the bottom of the pan with a wooden spoon to loosen any caramelized bits, until the vegetables are softened and lightly browned, about 10 minutes. Make a small clearing in the center, add the tomato paste, and cook, stirring, until fragrant and a bit darker, about 1½ minutes. Add the chicken broth, adjust the heat to medium-high, and bring to a strong simmer, again scraping the bottom of the pot to loosen and dissolve any additional caramelized bits. Add the browned lamb with the accumulated juices and stir to combine, submerging the lamb as much as possible. Return to a strong simmer.

Cover the pan, transfer to the oven, and bake for 1½ hours. Add ½ teaspoon salt, ½ teaspoon pepper, the carrot chunks, and potatoes, submerging them in the liquid as best you can. Replace the cover and continue to bake until the lamb and vegetables are very tender, 40 to 60 minutes longer. If the stew is more liquidy than you'd like, mash some of the potatoes against the side of the pot and stir them into the cooking liquid to thicken it.

Remove the bay leaves, add the vinegar, and stir to mix. Adjust the seasoning with additional salt and pepper, if necessary. Add most of the parsley and stir to combine. Serve immediately, sprinkling each portion with the remaining parsley.

COOK'S NOTE

If you can't find boneless lamb shoulder roast, you can substitute lamb shoulder blade chops and remove the bones. But in that case, buy extra.

Blood of Vol

SERVES 4

7 tablespoons extra-virgin olive oil

4 ounces thinly sliced salami or other cured sausage, cut into thin strips

1 large yellow onion, chopped

5 large red bell peppers, cored, seeded, and thinly sliced

1 bay leaf

Kosher salt

4 garlic cloves, thinly sliced

1½ teaspoons paprika

1 teaspoon minced fresh thyme

½ teaspoon red pepper flakes

One 14½-ounce can whole peeled tomatoes, drained and crushed by hand into small pieces, with ¼ cup juices reserved

1 teaspoon sherry vinegar

⅓ cup chopped fresh parsley

Freshly ground black pepper

8 eggs

In the military nation of Karnath, the faith known as the Blood of Vol symbolizes the inherent divinity within all people, stressing the power and comfort of the bonds that we form in this life. Exactly how the name of that religion became attached to this Eberron dish is a bit obscure—but the first bite you take will send divine strength coursing through your veins. The egg base is chock-full of sausage, onions, bell peppers, and enough spices to purify the soul—or in some cases, make you feel the flames of damnation, if there is such a thing. Some establishments serve this with an absolutely scorching amount of pepper, and its devotees settle for nothing less.

Line a plate with paper towels.

In a large nonstick skillet over medium heat, warm 3 tablespoons of the olive oil until shimmering. Add the salami and cook, stirring frequently, until lightly browned, about 3 minutes. With a slotted spoon, transfer the salami to the prepared plate and set aside, leaving the oil in the skillet. Add the onion, bell peppers, bay leaf, and 1 teaspoon salt to the skillet. Adjust the heat to medium-high and cook, stirring frequently, until the bell peppers are tender-crisp, about 20 minutes. Clear the center of the skillet, add 1½ tablespoons olive oil, and let warm for a moment. Add the garlic, paprika, thyme, and red pepper flakes and cook, stirring just those aromatics, until fragrant, about 45 seconds. Add the cooked salami and tomatoes with the reserved juices and stir to incorporate along with the aromatics into the bell peppers. Adjust the heat to medium and cook, stirring occasionally, until the flavors meld, about 5 minutes longer.

Remove the bay leaf; add the vinegar, most of the parsley, and ½ teaspoon salt; season with pepper; and stir to blend. Adjust the seasoning with additional salt and pepper, if necessary. Transfer the mixture to a serving dish and set aside. Wipe out the skillet with paper towels.

In a medium bowl, combine the eggs, 1½ tablespoons olive oil, ¾ teaspoon salt, and ½ teaspoon pepper and whisk until uniformly yellow.

Adjust the heat to medium, add the remaining 1 tablespoon olive oil to the skillet, and warm until shimmering. Add the egg mixture and cook, without stirring, for 20 seconds. Using a flexible heatproof spatula, scramble the eggs by scraping along the bottom and sides of the skillet and folding them in large strokes until clumped in large curds and just slightly wet, about 2 minutes longer. Immediately scrape the eggs over the pepper mixture in the serving dish. Sprinkle with the remaining parsley before serving.

BREADED BIRD CUTLETS

SERVES 4

Kosher salt and freshly ground black pepper

½ cup all-purpose flour

2 eggs

1 tablespoon water

4 skinless, boneless chicken breasts (about 7 ounces each), tenderloins removed, trimmed of fat

⅓ cup neutral oil

⅓ cup extra-virgin olive oil

3 tablespoons unsalted butter, cold

¼ cup minced shallot

2 teaspoons minced fresh thyme

½ cup dry vermouth or dry white wine

1 cup low-sodium chicken broth

½ lemon, thinly sliced

3 tablespoons minced fresh parsley

No one is quite sure how this crispy and succulent breaded chicken dish has proliferated across many planets of the multiverse, but *why* it appears on the menus of so many eateries is blatantly obvious—it's as classic as it is delicious. Traditional preparation of this multiversal main requires tenderizing and breading the cutlets to ensure that the chicken remains soft and moist. Each thin cutlet, the size of an orc's palm, is then fried in a flash to lock in the juices. Breaded Bird Cutlets are primarily served seasoned, lathered with butter, and spritzed with lemon, although breadings and sauces can vary greatly depending on the world and the occasion. If someone in your party is feeling adventurous, order a "stack"—three sizzling cutlets on a platter—which will surely satiate even the grandest appetite.

With a rack in the middle position, preheat the oven to 200°F. Place a wire rack on a large-rimmed baking sheet and set aside.

In a small bowl, combine 2½ teaspoons salt and 1 teaspoon pepper, stir to incorporate, and set aside.

Put the flour in a wide, shallow dish, such as a pie plate. In another wide, shallow dish, beat the eggs with the water. Set both dishes aside.

On a work surface, using a sharp knife, cut each chicken breast in half horizontally to make eight cutlets. Cover them with plastic wrap and use a meat pounder or the bottom of a small skillet to pound the thicker ends so the cutlets have an even thickness of ¼ to ½ inch. Remove the plastic, sprinkle the cutlets evenly with the salt-pepper mixture, and set aside to rest for 10 minutes.

Meanwhile, in a medium skillet over medium-high heat, combine the neutral oil and olive oil and warm until shimmering.

Dredge two cutlets in the flour on both sides and shake off the excess. Dip in the beaten egg mixture, allowing the excess to drip into the dish. Gently add the cutlets to the oil and cook until golden brown on the bottom, about 2 minutes (there should be active, but not violent, bubbling at the edges of the cutlets). Carefully flip them and cook until the second side is golden brown, about 2 minutes longer. Transfer the cutlets to the prepared wire rack, and put in the oven to keep warm. Repeat to cook the remaining cutlets, adjusting the heat if necessary to avoid burning (do not discard the remaining flour).

Discard the oil in the skillet, then carefully wipe it out with paper towels. Set the skillet over medium heat, add 1 tablespoon of the butter, and let melt, swirling to coat the bottom of the pan. Add the shallot, thyme, and ½ teaspoon salt and cook, stirring, until softened, about 2 minutes. Add the vermouth, adjust the heat to medium-high, and bring to a strong simmer. Cook, stirring and scraping the bottom of the pan with a wooden spoon to loosen and dissolve the caramelized bits, until the vermouth is reduced by almost half, about 2½ minutes. Add the chicken broth, lemon slices, and any juices accumulated from the rested cutlets. Return the mixture to a strong simmer, and cook, stirring occasionally, until again reduced by about almost half, about 3 minutes longer.

Meanwhile, cut the remaining 2 tablespoons butter into small cubes, add to the flour, and toss to coat. Remove the skillet from the heat, add the coated butter and ¼ teaspoon salt, season with pepper, and whisk to melt and incorporate the butter. Add the parsley and whisk to incorporate. Adjust the seasoning with additional salt and pepper, if necessary. Arrange the cutlets on a serving platter and spoon the sauce and lemon slices over them before serving.

HALFLING GAME BIRDS

SERVES 4

Kosher salt and freshly ground black pepper

1 tablespoon finely grated lemon zest

2 teaspoons minced fresh rosemary

2 teaspoons minced fresh thyme

2 Cornish game hens (about 2 pounds each)

Olive oil spray

Halflings may be small, but their love of fine food is known to be grand. It follows, then, that one of their most prized dishes would be correspondingly small of size but big on flavor, and such is the case with the dish called Halfling Game Birds. Rubbed with a secret mixture of rosemary, thyme, and lemon zest, these tasty Cornish hens are left to marinate overnight, testing the patience of many a halfling chef. When the waiting is over (almost never as long as is recommended), the birds are finally roasted at a scorching high heat to hasten them to the table where they never last long in front of eager diners. Whether Oerth, Toril, Eberron, or Krynn, these little game birds rule the roost on halfling tables across the multiverse.

Set a wire rack on a rimmed baking sheet and set aside.

In a small bowl, combine 1½ tablespoons salt, 1½ teaspoons pepper, the lemon zest, rosemary, and thyme; stir to incorporate; and set aside.

On a work surface, using kitchen or poultry shears, cut through both sides of, and remove, a Cornish hen's backbone. Repeat with the second hen. Working one at a time, turn the hens so they're breast-side up and then flatten with one of your hands. Using a chef's knife, cut through the breastbone to halve each hen.

Pat the hens dry with paper towels and then, working with one half hen at a time, gently shimmy a finger between the skin and the meat, loosening but not detaching the skin. Rub about one-fourth of the seasoning mixture under the skin of each half, then sprinkle about ½ teaspoon salt all over the skin of each half. Tuck the wing tips behind the breasts and arrange the halves skin-side up on the prepared rack. Refrigerate, uncovered, for at least 4 hours or up to 24 hours.

With racks in the upper-middle and lower-middle positions, place a second rimmed baking sheet on the lower rack, and preheat the oven to 500°F.

When the oven is ready, remove the hens from the refrigerator. Coat the skins with olive oil spray and sprinkle each hen half with about ¼ teaspoon pepper. Carefully arrange the hens, skin-side down, on the preheated baking sheet and roast for 10 minutes. Remove the hens from the oven and preheat the broiler. Flip the hens skin-side up, set the baking sheet on the upper rack, and broil the hens until well browned and an instant-read thermometer registers 160°F when inserted into the thickest part of a breast, and 175°F in the thickest part of a thigh, 6 to 9 minutes, rotating the sheet as necessary for even browning. Transfer the hen halves to a platter or individual plates. Serve immediately.

VADA'S VANILLA BUNS

MAKES 12 BUNS

1½ cups unsweetened flaked coconut

2½ cups bread flour, plus extra to dust the work surface

½ cup water, plus 1 tablespoon

3 vanilla beans

½ cup milk (not skim)

2 eggs

1 packet (2¼ teaspoons) instant or Rapid Rise yeast

¼ cup granulated sugar

Kosher salt

3 tablespoons unsalted butter, cut into 4 pieces and softened

COOK'S NOTES

When toasting the coconut, keep it moving in the skillet, and keep a close eye on it because it browns quickly once it begins and can burn easily. As soon as the coconut is browned to your liking, get it out of the hot skillet immediately.

The dough is quite soft and sticky, so a bowl scraper, ideally a flexible one, is very helpful for scraping it out of the mixer bowl (and off the dough hook) and forming the ball on the work surface prior to the first rise.

For those fortunate enough to visit the Radiant Citadel, a shining and otherworldly beacon of civilization deep in the Ethereal Plane, it is a nearly unrivaled cultural experience. Much more than a crossroads for weary interplanar pilgrims seeking passage to the founding civilizations of the Material Plane, the citadel is a veritable hub of flavors and cuisine all its own. The vanilla buns sold at Vada's Otherworldly Goods, made by the famous baker and Citadel resident Vada, are a scrumptious street-treat hailing from Siabsunkoh's famed Dyn Singh Market, nicknamed the Dancing Night Market due to its ever-shifting forms and truly magical and festive nature. These delicate rolled pastries are baked in a tightly packed bundle, resulting in a freshly cooked tray that resembles a bouquet of golden flowers. Crispy on the outside and cloudlike in the middle, these vanilla-flavored morsels don't last long at Vada's, or anywhere you find them, so be sure to grab one while you can. Although the original bun is crafted from a secret family recipe, this recipe is as close to the real thing as you are going to find.

In a medium skillet over medium heat, toast the coconut, stirring constantly, until many of the flakes are dark golden brown (some flakes will remain white, so the quantity will appear to be spotty brown), about 4 minutes. Immediately scrape the coconut into the bowl of a food processor, and set aside to cool to room temperature, at least 10 minutes. Pulse until it's about the texture of whole flax seeds (a little smaller than sunflower seeds), about five 2-second pulses, and set aside.

Meanwhile, carefully wipe out the still-hot skillet. In the skillet, off heat, whisk ¼ cup of the flour and ½ cup of the water until it forms a smooth, thick paste (with help from the residual heat in the skillet) about the texture of mashed potatoes, about 1 minute. Immediately scrape the paste into the bowl of a stand mixer, and set aside to cool until tepid, about 8 minutes.

Meanwhile, with a paring knife, halve the vanilla beans lengthwise and scrape the seeds from all six halves. Collect the seeds in a small dish, cover, and set aside.

Add the milk to the flour paste and whisk until smooth. Add one egg and whisk to incorporate it. Add the remaining 2¼ cups flour and the yeast. Fit the bowl and the dough hook to the stand mixer and mix on low speed for 1 minute. Adjust the speed to medium-low and continue mixing until the flour is incorporated and the resulting mass is cohesive, about 30 seconds longer. Turn off the mixer and rest the dough for 15 minutes. Add the sugar and 1½ teaspoons salt and knead on CONTINUED →

medium-low speed for 5 minutes, until the dough appears smoother. With the mixer running, add one piece of the butter and continue mixing until it is incorporated fully into the dough, about 30 seconds, before adding the next. Repeat to add and incorporate the remaining three pieces of butter, adding the vanilla seeds along with the last piece. Continue to mix on medium-low speed 5 minutes longer, adding the coconut midway through that time and stopping when needed to scrape down the dough hook and sides of the bowl (the dough will be quite soft and sticky).

Flour a work surface very lightly, scrape the dough from the bowl to the surface, and knead it briefly to form a ball. Lightly oil a medium bowl, add the dough, and turn it to coat very lightly with the oil. Cover the bowl with a clean kitchen towel or plastic wrap and set aside until the dough has become puffy and its volume has increased by three-fourths or doubled, about 1 hour.

Oil a 9-inch round cake pan, line the bottom with parchment paper, and oil the parchment paper. Transfer the dough to the work surface, gently deflate it, and press and stretch it into a 10 by 12-inch rectangle with a short side facing you. Cut the dough lengthwise into 4 equal strips and cut each strip crosswise into 3 equal pieces. Working with 1 piece of dough at a time, stretch and press the dough gently to form an 8 by 2-inch strip. Starting on a short side, roll the strip to form a snug cylinder. Arrange the shaped buns seam-side down in the prepared pan, placing 10 buns around the edge of the pan, pointing inward, and the remaining 2 buns in the center. Cover the pan with a clean kitchen towel or plastic wrap and set aside until the buns appear puffy and their volume has increased by about three-fourths or doubled, about 1 hour.

When ready to bake, with a rack in the lowest position, preheat the oven to 375°F. In a small bowl, beat the remaining egg with 1 tablespoon water. Gently brush the tops of the buns with the egg wash (take care not to deflate the dough) and bake until deep golden brown, 20 to 24 minutes, rotating the pan halfway through. Set the pan on a cooling rack and cool for about 15 minutes. Gently loosen the edges of the buns with your fingers and gently pry them out of the pan. Cool the buns until just warm or room temperature, remove the parchment from the bottom of the buns if necessary, and serve. Leftover buns can be wrapped tightly and stored at room temperature for up to 3 days.

RAY OF FROST

SERVES 2

Small ice cubes

4 ounces gin (such as London Dry)

½ ounce absinthe

⅓ ounce dry vermouth

2 lemon twists

This flavorful and strikingly cerulean concoction is said to chill its imbiber from the inside out. Named after the arcane incantation known for blasting its target with a rush of frigid energy and slowing their steps, ray of frost provides a cool option at upmarket taverns with more extensive and adventurous drink lists. Often served in a small crystal glass, Ray of Frost is an inspired blend of gin, absinthe, vermouth, and enough ice to chill even the coldest parts of Wildspace. The real challenge with this drink isn't surviving the initial icy brain-blast but surviving several glasses of it.

Chill two cocktail glasses, martini glasses, or coupes (see Cook's Note, page 92). Fill a large mixing glass about halfway with ice and add the gin, absinthe, and vermouth. Stir to blend and chill, about 30 seconds. Strain between the two chilled glasses. Run a lemon twist around the rim of each glass and drop it in before serving.

RUBY CORDIAL

SERVES 2

Small ice cubes

3 ounces ruby port

2 ounces brandy

½ ounce fresh lemon juice

⅓ ounce grenadine

2 lemon twists

2 cocktail cherries

Ruby cordial is traditionally a saccharine swill of liquefied dark cherries blended into a fortified wine from the southern Moonshae Islands, where the aperitif first originated. While any cherries will do, the cherries of choice originate from the same rustic archipelago where they ripen in the sandy island soil, which imbues them with a sweet, robust flavor. Distilling cherry stems, skins, and even pits into the liqueur activates an almost nutty layer of flavor that hits right after the initial sugary wave passes. The Blade and Stars, a tried-and-true establishment in the port city of Baldur's Gate, offers a remarkable interpretation of this offshore staple using a traditional ruby port instead of fermented Moonshae cherry juices. Even better, the Blade serves food and drink right in the guest rooms, ensuring that no one will notice just how many of these wondrous cocktails are consumed.

Fill two small rocks or old-fashioned glasses about halfway with ice. Fill a large cocktail shaker about halfway with ice and add the port, brandy, lemon juice, and grenadine. Cover and shake to blend and chill, about 30 seconds. Strain the mixture into each glass. Run a lemon twist around the rim of each glass, drop it in, and garnish with a cherry before serving.

RAVENLOFT

CRASH LANDING! Without a proper pilot, our heroes crash land the
SPELLJAMMER in foreboding BAROVIA! Grieving their lost friends, they
seek to finish their mission and deliver the poisoned wine, Veneno '18,
to a mysterious patron who lives in ominous CASTLE RAVENLOFT!

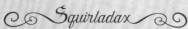

Squirladax

Disaster! The spelljammer, CRASHÈD near unknown woods! Dint's last squeaking command was that we abscond with the Veneno '18 and deliver it to the Castle Ravenloft!

We scream into the night and slink through misty shadows, wailing with every guilt-muddèd stride. In my quavering fingers, I hold chippèd RUBY, coughèd up there by dying Dint!

You see, we killed him! Only now do I understand. As the Veneno '18 poisoned sweet Bri'An, we too poisoned doughty Dint by pretending that Ruby, sweet Ruby, was the "Jewel of Javanium." (T'ever that 'tis!) As we devour beefs, so too did Dint consume gems for nourishment! He died, poisoned, believing we were some honest band of adventurers known as the Quaternate Tetrad. Even as he thrashed in painèd throes, he urged us forward to present ourselves to the Ravenloft patron and earn FIVE ASTRAL DIAMONDS.

My heart bleats in my ears as I lead my false Tetrad in flight: We scream unto the night!

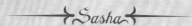

Sasha

After like an hour of screaming through the woods, I gained enough sense to pull myself together and slap Squirladax to non-screaming. I'm now pouring the local "Blood Meal" into his nose, which the manual suggests is the quickest way to restore warm blood directly to his brain.

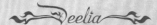

Deelia

Composure regained, I find Dint's murder . . . somewhat less fascinating now. I find this place, however, more appetizing. We are in a tavern called Blood on the Vine that is buried in the mist-shrouded village of "Barovia."

Barovia—a place of soulless eyes that both haunt and compel me.

Squirladax

At the tavern, I hunt Barovian Garlic Breads. I slay Fig Cakes with sharpened daggers o' the mouth. Sasha crunches Tavern Crickets. Oh, the leaps she'll make with cricket digestions greasing her leg hinges, so sayeth Volo's book.

Buoyed by Purple Grapemash No. 3, I realize Dint's memory must be honorèd. A false Tetrad playèd by a true triad will win the day! And Five Astral Diamonds they'll pay!

Amazing what a sauced paunch can do for morale. Veneno '18 in hand, I will now ask the taverneer what direction lies this friendly Castle Ravenloft!

Ugh, cursed reader! We now need to calm our "leader" Squirladax who fled the tavern wailing, after a misconstrued report from the tavern keeper.

Let me explain: The tavern host gnashed his teeth and brought fear to Squirladax's flapping ears with his words: "Castle Ravenloft is home to Strahd. The first Vampyr."

Upon hearing this, a'course, our little goblin man ran through the streets, screaming, "Vampeeeeer! Vampeeeer! We all die this night!"

How embarrassed 'twas he when I imparted to him of my superior knowledge of Shadow's Edge-ducation. (You see, in my studies with the Lords of Shadow's Edge, dark infernal worlds and secrets of the damned were revealed to me.)

I soothed fearful Squirladax that Vampeers is nothing to be a panic of. VamPIRES, to be sure! But Vampeers are simply contemporaries of equivalent stature and station as Vampires. For 'twere a Vampire to, say, be brought before a jury's court, the judgment would'st fall upon the vampire's Vampeers.

This calmed Squirladax; and cursèd goblin, he took the lead again.

His ignorance is astonishing.

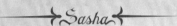

Oh, my breath bellows! We finally arrived at the top of the road, high above the moonlit countryside. Full moon, so that's creepy. . . . As was that wolf we passed that wore—I swear it was trousers? Chaps? Weird. Scary. . . . Sad. I've beat up my friends, lied, cheated, let another friend die, and applied my leeches under my eyes to suck my tears away. We now cross a drawbridge to the fog-swirled turrets of Castle Ravenloft.

The silence of your home is welcome, Strahd—absent as it is from the bothersome chit chat of servants. These chambers of black and purple are quiet as death. Were you expecting me? Will you entice me to betray my companions and send their dead souls to satisfy my Queen? What do you offer?

Oh—this prodigious feasting table that welcomes us! Roast Boar at one end, Two Hares Inn Rabbit Stew at the other. Baskets of Green Onion Pancakes and plates piled high with the sausages and potatoes of Quij's Plate. Carafes of Honeymilk towered above the rest! And in the marbled center, a space, no doubt, for the main course still to come! At the room's edge, there is a magnificent, gilded pipe organ, and behold on the opposite wall is a lavish portrait. . . . My new friend? Enemy? You **are** rather dashing, and I want to set your face aflame.

❧ Squirladax ❧

I watch as pallid, lanky, hairless men with idiot grins appear and perch themselves around us at the table. Eight in number, all of them silent smirking, and I do think, haughtily, at me. Do these **strangers**, conspiring to share a private jest, mean to belittle ME?! How dare?!

Oh wait . . .

While I have not trained under Lords of some fancy academy like Deelia, my memory jogs, and I now understand! These contemptible imbeciles are the deceased of humans oft referred to as "skeletons!" I do not know why these dead humans insist on smirking at me, though. What know'st they?

They must know that I am a murderer. My knees knock.

The walls groan, and a dust-encrusted, man-sized box is wheeled in by yet more condescending skeletons!

A ghostly voice emanates from lipless teeth. "Behold. He is Chahd." And the lid to what I now know is a coffin creaks open. I believe we are soon to meet our host.

❧ Deelia ❧

I report this from the water closet. Art thou yanking my leg? CHAHD?! Clambering clumsily from stupid coffin, highcollared velveteen cape, a plaster of yellow-moldy hair framing his round stupid face. I recognized him in an instant and hid to avoid his eyes.

Reader! Let Deelia blow thy wig bald.

He is NOT Chahd, nor Strahd! He is not vampire! This so-called Chahd is in reality CHAD, my old ally, turned nemesis. 'Twas HE that alerted the Lords of Shadow's Edge to exile me after a meager incident allegedly involving a small amount of purifying flame.

I must play my part, return to the banquet coolly, and challenge Chad's Vampyrity, for I doubt very much any vampire would see Chahd as peer.

❧ Squirladax ❧

We were feasting mirthfully, when—Chahd bellowed: "I AM VAMPIRE!" This caused a soiling of the pants of my very soul, when Deelia called out hence:

"You are neither Vampire, nor Vampeer, nor Chahd, but Chad! Where is the Lord of this Manor?"

Chahd bit back viciously. "He is gone afar for the weekend. A vacuum is left in this his house, his seat of power! And I am the sitter of this house!"

I retorted, "So your authority here is borrowed, not bought of wealth or influence?"

Chahd grinned evilly. "I have found a means of pyr review. Of buying my master's favor, my sweet Quaternate Tetrad." He gesticulated to the Veneno '18 and bade us drink deeply from it, for that 'twas its purpose all along!

"WELCOME TO MY MASTER'S BANQUET. FOR YOU SEE, YOU . . . ARE THE INGREDIENTS!"

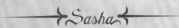

I DON'T GET ANYTHING! I WANNA GO HOME! Ok. . . . Sorry! First, I don't get why Deelia didn't just burn the hell out of Chahd, magicwise, but Chahd started calling her "Fire Fingers" and Deelia got something called "vexed!" The skeletons start pulling out GIANT CLEAVERS! I look to Squirladax, and he's crying into that stupid Ruby. . . .

Okay, so it's on me. Let's try to flip this table like they do in stage plays! Nope, it's too big. Then I started smashing plates, but no one cared. Wait! I'll bet that big expensive pipe organ would get Chahd in trouble if it were broken! So, I hurl my chair at it, and yeah! BOOM!! And SURPRISE. . . it shuddered and slid to reveal a FREAKING SECRET DOOR!

So that's when I smashed Chahd in the face with the Veneno and grabbed my friends. We ran like the wind!

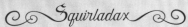

We flee into the eternal Barovian night and make it to the calamitous site beyond the woods where the spelljammer crashed. I can only guess, out of fear and madness, that we had some hope Dint would rise from his grave and whisk us and the spelljammer into the sky and to safety.

But then I remember . . BETRAYED! Dastardly Dint bade us deliver ourselves up to be eaten! Nary an Astral Diamond to be found! Now, out of the Svalich Woods, march the hungry skeletal minions of Vampeer housesitter, Chahd.

I sign off . . . from this life and deem this the final entry of the BUREAU OF DARK TABLES. TPK.

The skeletons will be here soon. Goodbye cruel universe, and hello to oblivion, as it is clear that I have not curried enough favor with the Queen to join her . . . in the Shadowfell.

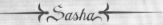

I am now super sad that I spent all my money on food instead of, like, a new battleaxe.

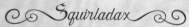
Squirladax

Boy, skeletons truly do march a snail's pace, do they not? With every step, however, my throat constricts, as I know this to be the end of all things. I see Chahd. He will drain my goblin blood. My death will be beyond all reasoning excruciation. 'Tis what I deserve. FIN.

Deelia

I wish I could make fire now so that I could make flame of myself, a screaming death. but Chahd has vexed me. I die vexed.

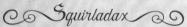
Squirladax

I just really think that as leaderpoet, it falls to me to end this journal proper, so it is with a heavy heart that . . . wait. What ho? Cresting the mountain to the west! A small, paunchy man with green draconic gait. I do not understand!

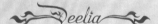
Deelia

OH, MY QUEEN! I GET IT! RAVENLOFT is IN THE SHADOWFELL! BEHOLD! OUR CLERIC BRI'AN IS SENT BY MY RAVEN QUEEN! HE HAS COME TO VANQUISH THE UNDEAD!

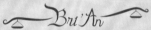
Bri'An

And so it 'twas that a whisper and a raven had whisked Bri'An away to the land of Shadows, but the Raven had an "oopsy" and brought the soul of Tyr's servant to RavenLOFT in-stead of the house of the Raven QUEEN. Tyr looked on and saw that 'twas fine. 'Twas an honest mistake.

So did'st Bri'An, son of Stev'An find himself the lone vanguard against the skeletal hordes. And Bri'An's friends begged weepily that Bri'An might perform a TURNING OF THE UNDEAD.

So he attempted the thing, with a fire of his dragonly voice, a raising of his holy hammer, and *I have no freaking-clue how that worked. Because, ok. Look. I'm a thief. My thing was that I was gonna' rob the goblin guy of that Ruby and use these fools as cover to rob the crap outta' more guys. I just thought it would be funny to pretend I'm a cleric.*

But when I raised my hammer, that Vampire guy looked at me, then looked at his skeleton friends, then looked back at me, screamed, and ran away.

So… I'm shook.

Tyr's REAL?

Tears in my eyes.

Halfling Iron Rations

MAKES ABOUT 4 CUPS

1 cup old-fashioned rolled oats

½ cup slivered almonds

½ cup coarsely chopped walnuts

½ cup raw pepitas

1½ tablespoons flaxseed

1½ tablespoons sesame seeds

1 egg white

3 tablespoons extra-virgin olive oil

1 teaspoon Worcestershire sauce

3 tablespoons packed light brown sugar

1 tablespoon minced fresh thyme

1½ teaspoons kosher salt

¾ teaspoon freshly ground black pepper

¾ teaspoon paprika

¾ teaspoon garlic powder

¾ teaspoon ground coriander

1 pinch cayenne pepper

COOK'S NOTE

Great as a snack, iron rations also make an excellent crunchy topping for thick soups such as Seelie Court Cheese and Potato Soup (page 191), salads, roasted vegetables, ratatouille, avocado toast, and deviled eggs.

B raving the dead wastes of the Shadowfell demands great preparation and fortitude. The endless gloom is unforgiving and yields little in the way of natural edible resources. Travelers would be wise to foreplan their meals and carry all required consumables with them. The iron rations prepared by Gloomwrought's surprisingly sizable halfling population are a notable and cost-effective trail treat. This creative medley of crushed nuts, local oats, and crunchy seeds are clumped into tiny balls and cemented with honey. And they are as packed with nutrients as they are yummy. Even when you're not embarking on an arduous, despair-filled journey, this granola makes for a nourishing, delectable snack that balances the sweet and savory.

With a rack in the middle position, preheat the oven to 325°F. Line a rimmed baking sheet with parchment paper or a nonstick baking mat and set aside.

In a medium bowl, combine the oats, almonds, walnuts, pepitas, flaxseed, and sesame seeds and stir to mix. In another medium bowl, combine the egg white, olive oil, Worcestershire, brown sugar, thyme, salt, black pepper, paprika, garlic powder, coriander, and cayenne and whisk vigorously until well blended. Pour the liquid mixture over the dry mixture and, using a flexible spatula, fold and stir until all the dry ingredients are well coated. Scrape the seed-oat mixture into the center of the prepared baking sheet and, using a large metal spatula, spread and firmly press into an even layer, roughly ⅜ inch thick (the shape is unimportant). The mixture will stick to the spatula as you work—simply scrape it off and continue.

Bake the granola until golden brown in the center and a little darker around the edges, about 25 minutes, rotating the pan about halfway through. Using the metal spatula, turn the granola; it will break into shards as you work, which is fine, but try to keep them as large as possible. Redistribute the granola into an even layer and continue to bake until it is deep golden brown, about 5 minutes longer. Let the granola cool to room temperature on the baking sheet (it will crisp further as it cools). If desired, break it into smaller pieces.

Store the granola in an airtight container at room temperature for up to 2 weeks.

TAVERN CRICKETS

MAKES 3 CUPS

1½ tablespoons chile-lime seasoning (such as Tajín)

2 teaspoons garlic powder

½ teaspoon cayenne pepper

Kosher salt and freshly ground black pepper

1 cup roasted and salted peanuts

1 cup raw pepitas

1 cup whole roasted crickets

2 tablespoons unsalted butter, melted

There is an old phrase popular among the dwellers of the Shadowfell: "Choice is for the spoilt." Perhaps that idiom is the origin of this modest and practical insect-based recipe that dates back centuries and speaks to the ingenuity of the plane's original inhabitants. Adult crickets are flash-fried, air-dried, and then seasoned with an assortment of aromatics, including chile, lime, and cayenne, and are served by the dozen in a large rolled-leaf "cone." As popular in the Material Plane of Faerûn as they are in the Shadowfell, tavern crickets are a crunchy, irresistibly tangy, protein-packed snack that can brighten the otherwise dismal days spent in the region.

With a rack in the middle position, preheat the oven to 300°F. Line a large rimmed baking sheet with parchment paper or a nonstick baking mat.

In a small bowl, combine the chile-lime seasoning, garlic powder, cayenne, ½ teaspoon salt, and ½ teaspoon black pepper and whisk to incorporate. Set aside.

In a large bowl, combine the peanuts, pepitas, and crickets and stir to blend. Add the melted butter, stir, and toss to coat the mixture evenly. Add the spice mixture and toss again to coat. Evenly spread the mixture on the prepared baking sheet.

Bake the crickets until dry and fragrant, about 20 minutes, stirring well three times during the baking time. Adjust the seasoning with additional salt and pepper, if necessary. Let cool to room temperature.

Tavern Crickets can be stored in an airtight container at room temperature for up to 1 week.

Barovian Garlic Bread

MAKES 12 KNOTS

4 tablespoons unsalted butter

2 tablespoons pressed or grated garlic

1½ teaspoons water

Kosher salt

All-purpose flour for dusting

1 pound pizza dough, at room temperature

This buttery bread, served in both loaf and knot form, is ever-present in the taverns and inns dotting the misty (and eerie) Barovian countryside. While it's not uncommon for wayward travelers to get the cold shoulder from reclusive and suspicious denizens, inns such as the Blue Water will at least offer a warm basket of this local treat to well-mannered and paying patrons. It is important to note that although garlic is a flavorful and inspired touch, it is not indigenous to the region. You'll find this pungent bread pairs nicely with a main of medium-rare wolf steak and a glass of Wizard of Wines' Champagne du le Stomp or Red Dragon Crush, but avoid the Purple Grapemash No. 3 at all costs.

With a rack in the upper-middle position, preheat the oven to 475°F. Line a large rimmed baking sheet with parchment paper or a nonstick baking mat, place a wire rack on the baking sheet, and set aside.

In a small saucepan over medium-low heat, melt 2 tablespoons of the butter; add the garlic and water; and cook, stirring frequently, until the garlic is pale gold and very fragrant, 8 to 10 minutes. Add the remaining 2 tablespoons butter and stir to melt. Remove the pan from the heat and let the mixture rest to infuse with the garlic flavor, about 10 minutes.

Set a fine-mesh strainer over a small, microwave-safe bowl and strain the garlic butter, pressing on the solids to squeeze out as much butter as possible. Stir ½ teaspoon salt into the butter and set aside.

Generously dust a work surface with flour. Put the pizza dough on the surface and shape into a 12-inch log. Using a bench knife, cut the log crosswise into quarters and then cut each quarter into thirds. Roll each of the twelve dough pieces into an 8- to 9-inch rope and tie each rope into a simple knot. Tuck the ends underneath the knot. Place the knots, about 2 inches apart, on the prepared rack.

Bake the knots until they are just set, about 5 minutes. Remove from the oven and brush with half the garlic butter. Rotate the baking sheet 180 degrees from its original position, return to the oven, and continue baking until the knots are lightly browned on the top, about 7 minutes longer. (Meanwhile, if the remaining garlic butter has hardened, microwave it for about 15 seconds at partial power to melt.) Remove the knots from the oven and immediately brush them with the remaining garlic butter. Sprinkle lightly with salt, let cool for 5 minutes, and then serve warm.

GREEN ONION PANCAKES

SERVES 3 TO 4 AS AN APPETIZER

⅓ cup all-purpose flour

2 teaspoons onion powder

½ teaspoon baking powder

Kosher salt and freshly ground
black pepper

⅓ cup crème fraîche (see Cook's Note)

1½ tablespoons whole milk or
half-and-half, plus more as needed

1 egg, beaten

¼ cup very cold water, plus more
as needed

1½ teaspoons soy sauce

1½ tablespoons neutral oil

½ cup finely shredded green cabbage,
massaged with your hands to soften

1 small carrot, peeled and grated on
the large holes of a box grater

16 scallions, trimmed, whites thinly
sliced and greens cut into 2-inch
lengths

When the great floating enclaves of the Netheril Empire came crashing down, so, too, did their culinary secrets. But one community survived by escaping to the Shadowfell, and with it one of their most prized recipes was preserved: Green Onion Pancakes. While the Netherese, now known as the shadowstuff-infused Shadovar, have changed much over the centuries, this spectacular dish hasn't. These allium-based pancakes are an inexpensive and unexpectedly filling treat that pairs easily with savory roast meats. They're also delicious served solo, when dolloped with fresh cream and pureed fig spread for a uniquely Netherese experience. In many regions, scallions are an equally acceptable base vegetable that offers a pancake with a milder flavor. Regardless of how one chooses to consume this pan-fried appetizer, the culinary experience is one of the few good reasons to come to the Shadowfell.

With a rack in the middle position, preheat the oven to 250°F. Set a wire rack in a rimmed baking sheet and set aside.

In a small bowl, combine the flour, onion powder, baking powder, and 1½ teaspoons salt; season with pepper; whisk to incorporate; and set aside.

In a medium bowl, combine the crème fraîche and milk and whisk to a thick, barely pourable consistency, adding more milk, about 1 teaspoon at a time, as needed. Using a flexible spatula, scrape the mixture into a small serving dish and put in the refrigerator.

In the medium bowl, combine the egg, water, soy sauce, and 1½ teaspoons of the neutral oil and whisk until well blended. Add the flour mixture and whisk to form a loose, smooth batter with the consistency of applesauce, adding more water by the teaspoon (up to 4 teaspoons), if necessary. Add the cabbage, carrot, and scallions; mix to coat the vegetables with batter; and let rest for about 5 minutes.

In a medium nonstick skillet over medium heat, warm 1½ teaspoons neutral oil until shimmering. Stir the batter mixture, add half of it to the skillet, and immediately spread it into a roughly 7-inch round. Cook, undisturbed, until well browned on the bottom, about 3½ minutes. With a rubber spatula, flip the pancake and cook the second side, adjusting the heat if necessary, until the second side is spotted with brown, about 3½ minutes longer. Transfer the pancake to the prepared rack and place in the oven to keep warm. Add the remaining 1½ teaspoons neutral oil to the skillet, warm until shimmering, and repeat to cook the remaining batter into a second pancake. Transfer the pancake from the oven to a plate, add the second pancake, and set them aside to cool for about 4 minutes. Cut the pancakes into wedges and serve with the crème fraîche mixture.

TWO HARES INN RABBIT STEW

SERVES 4

8 bone-in, skin-on chicken thighs (2½ to 3 pounds), trimmed and dried well with paper towels

Kosher salt and freshly ground black pepper

2 tablespoons neutral oil

1 pound cremini mushrooms, wiped clean and quartered (small ones halved)

2 medium yellow onions, halved pole to pole and each half thinly sliced lengthwise

2 bay leaves

2½ teaspoons pressed or grated garlic

2 teaspoons minced fresh thyme, or 1 teaspoon dried

2 teaspoons minced fresh oregano or rosemary

1½ tablespoons all-purpose flour

¾ cup dry white wine

One 14½-ounce can diced tomatoes, drained

¾ cup low-sodium chicken broth

⅓ cup chopped fresh parsley

It should come as no surprise that the signature dish of the Two Hares Inn, located on the zombie-infested Barovian island of Sourange, is a rabbit stew prepared with one of the region's many famous wines. What's more surprising is who makes it, for it is said about the proprietor and chef that even death "hasn't interfered with his talent." It's a classic example of not wanting to know how the sausage, or in this case, stew—a delicious medley infused with intricate notes of thyme, oregano, and dry white wine—is made. In regions where rabbit isn't available, chicken has become a popular (and, in many cases, preferred) substitute. Whichever protein you cook, it is sure to reanimate your taste buds.

Sprinkle the chicken thighs all over with salt and pepper.

In a large sauté pan or Dutch oven over medium-high heat, warm 1 tablespoon of the neutral oil until shimmering. Arrange half the chicken thighs skin-side down in the pan, adjust the heat to medium, and cook, undisturbed, until the skin is browned, about 5 minutes. Flip the chicken and continue to cook, undisturbed, until the second side is browned, about 5 minutes longer (adjust the heat if necessary to avoid scorching). Transfer the chicken to a large plate. Repeat to brown the remaining chicken thighs. When the chicken is cool enough to handle, remove and discard the skin. Remove and discard all but 1½ tablespoons of the fat from the pan.

Adjust the heat to medium-high, add the mushrooms and ¼ teaspoon salt to the pan, and cook, stirring occasionally, until the mushrooms release their liquid and it evaporates, 7 to 10 minutes. Add the onions, bay leaves, and ¼ teaspoon salt and cook, stirring occasionally, until the mushrooms brown and the onions soften, about 4 minutes longer. Adjust the heat to medium; add the garlic, thyme, oregano, and flour; and cook, stirring constantly, until fragrant and the flour films the bottom of the pan, about 1 minute longer. Add the wine, adjust the heat to high, and bring to a simmer, stirring and scraping the bottom of the pan with a wooden spoon until the film of browned flour dissolves into and thickens the liquid, about 1 minute longer. Add the tomatoes and chicken broth, adjust the heat to medium-high, and bring to a boil. Add the chicken thighs with any accumulated juices and return to a simmer. Adjust the heat to low, cover, and let simmer gently until the chicken is cooked through and very tender, 35 to 45 minutes, flipping the chicken pieces about halfway through. Transfer the chicken to a serving platter, tent loosely with aluminum foil to keep warm, and set aside.

Remove the pan from the heat. Let the braising liquid rest for about 5 minutes, remove the bay leaves, and spoon off as much fat as possible (or use a fat separator). Set the pan over medium-high heat, add any accumulated juices from the chicken, bring to a boil, and cook, stirring occasionally, until reduced slightly, about 4 minutes longer. Adjust the seasoning with additional salt and pepper, if necessary. Stir in most of the parsley. Pour the sauce over and around the chicken. Sprinkle with the remaining parsley before serving.

WHOLE ROAST BOAR

SERVES 8 TO 10

3 tablespoons light brown sugar

3 tablespoons kosher salt

1 tablespoon freshly ground black pepper

One 8-pound whole bone-in pork butt (also known as shoulder butt), skinned, with fat cap attached

2 to 3 cups water, plus more as needed

PORT SAUCE

2 tablespoons reserved pork fat (from above)

½ cup minced shallots

1 tablespoon chopped fresh thyme

Kosher salt

2 tablespoons tomato paste

1 cup ruby port

¾ cup low-sodium chicken broth

2 tablespoons red currant jam

2 tablespoons unsalted butter

1½ teaspoons sherry vinegar

Freshly ground black pepper

Whole roast boar, or some parts thereof, is a favorite at the banquets of vampire hosts throughout the Domains of Dread. It is rumored that hosts wait until their guests are "glassy of eye, greasy of chin, and a drowsy cheer has come upon them" to insert a single fang to the jugular of each guest and exsanguinate to their taste. Proper preparation requires of the cook an unabashed love of jam, port, and brown sugar, applied with a heavy hand to flavor the meat, ensuring that you and your guests will leave nothing on your plates. For those lucky travelers fortunate enough to escape the fog-shrouded confines of Barovia to Toril, a variation of this hearty and succulent feast is a specialty of the Boar with Black Tusks in Noanar's Hold, which sometimes uses pork when a boar cannot be procured and is often served with a dry ruby wine from Cormyr.

In a small bowl, combine the brown sugar, salt, and pepper and whisk to blend. Using a very sharp knife, cut slits about 1 inch apart in a crosshatch pattern across the entire fat cap of the pork, taking care to cut all the way through the layer of fat, but not into the meat beneath it. Sprinkle the brown sugar–salt mixture all over the pork, making sure to rub it into the slits. Wrap the meat tightly in plastic wrap and refrigerate for at least 12 hours or up to 24 hours.

With a rack in the lowest position, preheat the oven to 325°F. Coat a roasting rack with nonstick cooking spray and set it in a large roasting pan.

Unwrap the pork and, with paper towels, blot the surface dry and remove any excess salt mixture if it hasn't completely dissolved. Place the pork on the prepared roasting rack, fat cap–side up, and pour the water into the pan, making sure it does not touch the bottom of the pork. Roast until the pork is very tender (a paring knife should slip in and out of the meat very easily) and the meat near the bone (but not touching it) registers 190°F on an instant-read thermometer, about 5 hours, checking once or twice on the water level in the roasting pan. If there is less than ¾ cup, add more. Transfer the pork to a platter or carving board, cover loosely with aluminum foil, and let rest for 30 minutes. Pour the liquid from the roasting pan into a fat separator or a narrow, heatproof container, and allow it to settle for 10 minutes. Set aside 2 tablespoons of the fat for the sauce and discard the rest.

If desired, make extra-crisp cracklings by raising the oven temperature to 475°F and returning the rested pork to the roasting pan, fat cap–side up. Roast until the cracklings are dark, blistered, and crisp, 8 to 10 minutes,

CONTINUED →

WHOLE ROAST BOAR CONTINUED

rotating the pan halfway through. Return the pork to the platter or carving board, cover loosely with foil, and let rest for 15 minutes longer.

Cut the pork into thick slices, or using a fork, gently pull apart into small chunks. Arrange on a serving platter and cover with foil until the sauce is finished.

To make the port sauce: In a medium skillet over medium heat, warm the reserved pork fat until shimmering. Add the shallots, thyme, and ½ teaspoon salt and cook, stirring, for 1 minute. Add the tomato paste and cook, stirring, until fragrant and a shade darker, about 1½ minutes. Add the port, adjust the heat to medium-high, and bring to a strong simmer. Cook, stirring occasionally, until reduced by a little less than half, about 3 minutes. Add the chicken broth (and any juices accumulated from the rested pork), return the mixture to a strong simmer, and cook, stirring occasionally, until reduced again by slightly less than half, about 3 minutes longer. Adjust the heat to medium, add the jam, and whisk vigorously until dissolved and incorporated. Remove the skillet from the heat, add the butter and vinegar, and whisk to incorporate. Season generously with pepper and whisk to incorporate. Adjust the seasoning with additional salt and pepper, if necessary.

Serve the pork and sauce together.

QUIJ'S PLATE

SERVES 4

3 tablespoons neutral oil

1 pound fresh sausage (your choice of flavor), casings removed

2 pounds red or all-purpose potatoes, cut into ½-inch cubes

Kosher salt

⅓ cup water

2 medium yellow onions, chopped

1 large red bell pepper, cored, seeded, and chopped

1 tablespoon chopped fresh sage, or 2 teaspoons minced fresh thyme or rosemary

1½ teaspoons pressed or grated garlic

¼ cup half-and-half

Freshly ground black pepper

½ cup chopped fresh parsley

4 eggs

Quij's Plate, consisting of pan-fried sausage, twice-browned potatoes, and eggs, is a filling meal that infallibly populates the menus of countless caravan cooks. Easy to prepare on the road for large parties, it has also become a popular dish in the military for its simplicity and heartiness to help soldiers brave the endless grey days. Named after an orc henchman of Lord Robilar, who inventively cooked this sausage meal for his adventuring party, using his shield for a skillet, Quij's Plate would eventually earn its place on the menu of the famed Green Dragon Inn, nestled in the Free City of Greyhawk's bustling River Quarter. The unusual name has since become the catch-all term for the countless iterations of this sausage-and-potato-based campfire classic, including those that migrated to misty Barovia via lost and hungry adventurers.

In a large skillet (preferably cast iron) over medium heat, warm 1 tablespoon of the neutral oil until shimmering. Add the sausage and cook, stirring and breaking it into small pieces, until it no longer appears raw, 3 to 4 minutes. With a slotted spoon, transfer the sausage to a bowl or plate, leaving behind the rendered fat.

In the same skillet over medium heat, warm the remaining 2 tablespoons neutral oil with the sausage fat until shimmering. Add the potatoes and ¼ teaspoon salt and stir to coat the potatoes with the oil and fat. Add the water, cover, and cook until the potatoes are just tender, 12 to 14 minutes. Uncover the skillet; add the onions, bell pepper, and ½ teaspoon salt; and cook, stirring frequently, until softened and light golden, about 8 minutes. Add the sage and garlic and cook, stirring, until fragrant, about 40 seconds. Add the half-and-half, 1 teaspoon salt, and black pepper to taste, stirring until well blended. Pat the mixture flat in the pan, adjust the heat to medium-high, and cook, undisturbed, until the visible moisture evaporates, there is no more visible bubbling on the surface, and the bottom begins to brown, 8 to 10 minutes. Using a wooden spoon or a stiff spatula, stir the mixture, scraping the brown bits from the bottom of the pan. Return the sausage to the pan and add most of the parsley, stirring to blend. Adjust the seasoning with additional salt and pepper, if necessary.

Using the back of a spoon, make an indentation for each egg, crack an egg into each, and sprinkle lightly with salt and pepper. Cover the skillet, adjust the heat to medium, and cook until the egg whites are set and the yolks are warm and slightly thickened but still liquid, 6 to 9 minutes, depending on how firm you like your eggs. Sprinkle with the remaining parsley before serving.

Fig Cakes

MAKES 6 CAKES

¾ cup slivered almonds, lightly toasted (see Cook's Note, page 24) and cooled

8 ounces dried figs, quartered

1½ teaspoons finely grated lemon zest

¾ teaspoon ground cinnamon

¾ teaspoon ground anise

1 small pinch kosher salt

3 tablespoons brandy or cognac

⅓ cup sesame seeds, lightly toasted (see Cook's Note, page 24) and cooled

Fig cakes are an easily preserved pouch snack for explorers with a sweet tooth. A perfect fig cake is as much about the fig as it is about the lightly toasted and ground almonds that form this fruity confection's chewy base. While honeyed fig tarts were extremely popular in Calimshan on the planet Toril, it is believed that this unique dessert originally hailed from the desolate wastes of the Shadowfell. Developed by the elves native to the Plane of Shadow called the Shadar-Kai, these treats are sweet enough to be at home even in the dreamy Feywild. In addition to the sesame seeds and anise seeds, a strong brandy is often infused into the mix, to both sweeten and fortify these small pressed cakes. While fig cakes do not come cheap, they are, nonetheless, a proud (and delicious) reminder of the resourcefulness of the Shadar-Kai.

In a food processor, pulse the almonds until fine but not pasty, about five 2-second pulses. Scrape the ground nuts into a medium bowl. Add the figs, lemon zest, cinnamon, anise, salt, and brandy to the food processor and process until very finely chopped and well blended, about 20 seconds, stopping to scrape down the sides as necessary. Add the ground almonds and pulse several times to incorporate them, about four 2-second pulses. Scrape the mixture into the medium bowl. Place the sesame seeds in a wide, shallow bowl.

Roll scant ¼-cup portions of the mixture into six balls, gently pressing as you roll to help them cohere. Press gently with your fingers to flatten and shape the balls into ovals about 3 inches long, 2 inches wide, and ½ inch thick. Working with one oval at a time, place it in the sesame seeds, pressing gently to help the seeds adhere to the bottom. Place the cakes, sesame-side up, on a plate. Let rest to firm up and dry out slightly, for 1 hour before serving.

Honey Milk

MAKES 4 CUPS

4 cups whole milk
1½ tablespoons honey

Frequently enjoyed by the Shadovar as a nightcap or a light dessert, honey milk is traditionally a stand-alone beverage that can be served chilled, warm, or even as toddy, spiked with herbal liqueur (as it is frequently done in the Shadowfell's forsaken city of Gloomwrought). While the preparation of honey milk is quite simple, the best versions balance a modest amount of honey with the freshest dairy (often imported from the Prime Material Plane) to produce a hearty yet refreshing drink served to all ages. However, the true key to properly preparing honey milk is patience. Traditionally, shadovar alchemists allow the mixture to marinate and cool for several hours before serving, and often include a garnish of cinnamon or citrus to make an attractive presentation for this lovely libation. Its elixir-like qualities are whispered to be good on the gut.

In a medium saucepan over medium heat, combine the milk and honey and bring to a bare simmer, stirring to dissolve the honey. Remove from the heat and let the mixture cool until barely warm. Pour it into a container with a tight-fitting lid and seal. Refrigerate until cold, about 3 hours, before serving.

PURPLE GRAPEMASH No. 3

SERVES 2

4 ounces white or amber rum

1 ounce fresh lime juice, plus
2 lime slices

½ cup grape jelly

2 cups small ice cubes

COOK'S NOTE

*To chill a sturdy wine glass, put it in
the freezer for an hour before using.*

Barovia is known for many things, its wine among them. The Wizard of Wines Vineyard is legendary for producing some of the finest wines throughout the planes and multiverse, such as the full-bodied Red Dragon Crush and the crisp Champagne du le Stomp. But not all wines that emerge from the mists of Barovia are of equal quality, as evidenced by the existence of Purple Grapemash No. 3. Priced at only three copper pieces per pint at most local taverns and other Domains of Dread, this table wine is known to be spectacularly unremarkable. However, in some areas of the Shadowfell, clever mixologists have added copious amounts of ice and lime juice to the pungent grape-ish mix, turning this otherwise mediocre concoction into a refreshing, slushy treat worth at least four copper pieces anywhere.

Chill two sturdy wine glasses, stemmed or not, or margarita glasses.

In a blender, combine the rum, lime juice, grape jelly, and ice cubes and blend until the ice is finely crushed and the mixture is uniform, slushy, and moves easily in the blender jar (the timing will depend on the power of your blender). Divide the mixture between the prepared glasses, garnish each with a lime slice, and serve immediately, with straws, if desired.

SIGIL

Having barely escaped Chahd's cruelty in RAVENLOFT, and with the help of Tyr's holy servant, our heroes fling themselves through secret portals and magical gateways of the multiversal planescape into SIGIL, the fabled CITY OF DOORS!

❧ Squirladax ❧

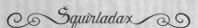

Treason. Doors, and more doors. But the final door, fearful reader, has been finally unbolted to the darkest basement in a goblin's heart.

On yesternight, Bri'An, fresh from his miracle, plucked Dint from the ruined spelljammer, and piously unburdened a (surprising) meal of gemstone treasures into Dint's greedy gullet. Sparked to life did Dint angrily, and with shaking fist, coughed indignities meant to soil our honor!

And then HE RAN! "AFTER HIM!" I cried!

And would'st thou be shocked to learn that Dint KNEW PRECISELY how to flee the mist-shrouded lands where Chahd's treason and Dint's betrayal make spouse, wedded in unholy union against us. But now, through many portals of smoke and magic and strange hidden doors, we hath apprehended he! Seized Dint, our tormentor!

It is now under the topsies and turvies of the strangest city, in a dank morgue cellar, that Dint awaits justice, strapped thusly in a chair by iron rings in this cold forgotten vault. Here, the flames of treason burn dimly, and for the last time, in the glassy lenses of Dint's mocking helmet.

✦ Sasha ✦

Squirladax has lost it. He's currently . . . fighting a mop, tugging at its moppy hairs!

❧ Deelia ❧

I have powdered with flour Squirladax's mop-wig. He now has the countenance of a distinguished minister of a house of justice. We now defer to the traditions of the legal system!

Followed by execution of Dint. Obviously.

❧ Squirladax ❧

ON THIS DAY, YEAR OF TYR'S JUDGMENT, TODAY, THE TRIAL OF DINT THE BETRAYER, MASTER OF TREASON, SHALL NOW BEGIN. WE WILL COMMENCE BY REMOVING THE BRONZE PLATEMAIL OF THE BETRAYER SO THAT A PURIFYING FLAMBEAU MAY BE APPLIED TO HIS SOOTED TONGUE TO BURN THE LIES FROM OUT HIS MOUTH! IN TYR'S NAME!

❧ Deelia ❧

I delighted at the prospect of whispering Dint's soul to the Nine Hells, but now I am aghast, as the peeling of the bronze helm yields a CLOCKWORK MAN! An autognome with many gyres and gears for guts!

"More lies!" screams forth Judge Squirladax, "as Dint assured us that he was an 'Otter Gnome'!"

Hardly surprising that the Master of Treason has neither otter nor gnome inside his bronze skull! Heretic! BURN HE NOW WITH THE FIRES OF THE RAVEN QUEEN!

. . . . Which I would summon were I not still vexed.

Many damns upon you, Chahd!

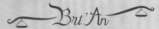

And so 'twas that Tyr's uneasy servant watched that Judge Squirladax called forth his first witness, "Dint. Architect of Treason, Master of Puppets," as christened by our judge and leader.

"Did not you, so-called 'Otter Gnome,' promise us FIVE ASTRAL DIAMONDS in payment of our questing?!"

And so rasped Dint, "Yes, goblin. But as the QUATERNATE TETRAD was not delivered to the customer, Master Chahd surely bequeathed a ONE. ASTRAL. DIAMOND. REVIEW."

"Ah! And you think you can abate the wrath of my RIGHTEOUS JUDGMENT by HIDING THIS DIAMOND? WHEREFORE 'TIS IT, PUPPET MASTER? I WILL HAVE THE TRUTH!" howled Judge Squirladax.

. . . All this talk of truth.

Ah! I have called lunch break, and I mull over my next inquisitings as we feast on Bacon-Wrapped Smoked Mussels and Fried Bread and Spices in pursuit of justice. Chahd the Betrayer of Deelia. Dint, the Puppet Master. Her **betrayer** linked to the strings of mine own **tormentor**. It all makes sense now, and as Dint puppeteers with malice, so too do I pull the strings righteously of my own companions.

Both us, short in stature. Both puppeteers. Dint is shadowy twin to mine self, thus making him my ARCH-NEMESIS. And how special a thing 'tis to have one's arch-nemesis in shackles and at the mercy of justice?

To think I ever felt guilt over having killed him.

I now drink this smoldering cup of Kaeth in exaltation. I think I shall have Sasha press the truth from him when we return.

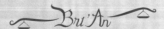

Tyr forgive me, for I could not stand by any longer! Deelia whooped many screeches of delight as Squirladax demanded back-breaking toils!

With every question, supine Sasha from a bench did press the poor squeaking Otter Gnome up off her chest in repetitions of eight! With Sasha suffering, now swollen armed and sopping, I knew I must act!

"BY TYR! I POISONED MYSELF!" I cried.

This did'st stop the screams and pressings.

"Poisoned we Dint first, with chippèd Ruby!" I howled.

This did'st earn a measure of widening from the judgmental goblin eyes!

"And FINALLY, did'st Tyr not witness our deception?! We are no Tetrad as we promised Dint!"

A shamed silence fell about every soul in that basement.

"Chahd withheld the Astral Diamonds because of OUR LIES! And if Dint has but one diamond, and this be HIS VERY FOOD. . . ."

A look of shame manifested on Deelia's demonic features.

"If we point greasy finger at HE, after our sumptuous lunching, might three equally greasy fingers be pointed back . . . at thee?!"

And Tyr looked and saw . . .

'Twas food for thinking.

Squirladax

Weeks have passèd since Dint's acquittal. 'Twas not finest my moment, but the legal system provèd sound and justice 'twas served. And served us well it did as we now swim in ASTRAL DIAMONDS! Twenty and one by my count!

How-fore thus?

Dint. He is a Fetch/Carry Questor. A deliverer of foods. Quest us with, say, Fire-Wrapped Golden Fish and bid us deliver these morsels to an address and so it shall be done. As reward, we accumulate Astral Diamonds. Now, plainly I have yet to caress one in mine own hand, but Dint's ledgers mark their birth, and we must first earn back a sum of diamonds equivalent to purchase he a new spelljammer to replace the demolished Dashor. Until then, deliver we the finest foods about the extra-planar bustle of Sigil, the mad City of Doors! I slow about the Great Bazaar of Sigil as Chirper's Sugar Biscuits beckon my goblin nose with the aromas of other-worldly spices.

I judgèd Dint a dark puppeteer. He is, instead, a kindly, and I think senseless, "Ahh—Tah—Muh—Tahn," what 'ere that is. But what am I, pulling at my minions' strings with glee?

Is this not my job?! . . . Why then does regret bitterly season my biscuits?

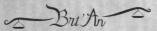

Bri'An

Tyr be praised! This band coins Astral Diamonds like a mint! Who knew piety could be so profitable! I ripped a sandwich in twain with my grinning fangs, then hurled the other half at a residential door! A TWENTY SECOND Astral Diamond is born! Huzzah!

Dint

Upon review of *Dungeons & Dining Digest*, that most authoritative periodical of culinary happenings, we have accrued twenty-two **One Astral Diamond Reviews**. Business is Non-Functional.

The squat cleric is egregious in his failed deliveries. I explain that a ONE DIAMOND RATING is FAILURE! He quips back "Tyr's bird is grasped in hand, and I care not how many twobirds lie in the bushels."

I calculate that our gross receipts equal 12 gold pieces. At this rate it will take two thousand and seventy-eight Sigil years to purchase a new spelljammer.

I am ruined.

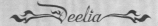

Deelia

The Shadowfell 'tis real. I whispered a soul to the afterlife, and so did'st my Queen smile. Will there be peace for me? Why then is there no fire in my breast? Why can'st I, even now, summon a drooping spark to warm the Emerald Chicken that I journey to deliver?

UGH! Be-cause VEXED!

Sour memories rise to torment me. My unjust expulsion from Shadow's Edge Academy. I only lit the kitchen of Shadow's Edge ablaze . . . Well, in truth the whole of the academy **IS** a kitchen. Shadow's Edge is a culinary magic academy, of course! The abyssal secrets of the sweetest meats and cheeses, it once held. The physical building no longer remains, however. Nor any trace. 'Tis the truth of fire.

Also true is that Chad betrayed me! Fled he wailing from the inferno, howling for the aid of the Shadow's Edge Lords! Whining, burning child! Tattler of tales!

How dare he! "Fiery Fingers," he taunts even now in my dreams! Curse he, pretender to vampire peer groups! He vexes me from his seat of house-sitting power in the very Shadowfell I wish to return to. Untouched and untouchable, he steals my flame from me even now.

Vexed.

Sasha

Demands! Dint has been trying to puppet master me into, get this, not tasting the foods that we deliver! First, he was all "You have to be on time!" And that's hard in the City of Doors! Cuz, if you walk through the wrong door, then you're like surrounded by this huge battle—a ranger and his party fighting a one-horned mage to save a baby unicorn, the cavalier wailing for help! Screw that! You run! Finally FIND the door, but it's NOT the door! It's a big, fake dragon head thing at a bizarro carnival! . . . So, turn back, right?

"You have to be on time!" but you're famished. So . . . you take a teeny little nibble, and you're a teeny, little late!

Squirladax says that food tasters were things that ROYALTY LOVED! We should be charging extra!

Bri'An

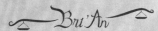

ATTACKÈD! Tyr forgive me! Sasha and I were about to celebrate our twenty-third Astral Diamond over some Sensate Palate Cleanser when ghastly skeletons boiled up from sewer plates, clambered clickity out of windows and from miasmal alleyways! By Tyr, I could see the purple and red velveteen cape, standing atop a dark minaret, a pate of pasted blonde hair, smiling brighter than even the skeletal hordes! Chahd!

Sasha looked to me, a glittering hope upon her scabbèd, leech-suckèrd face.

And thusly I drew my holy hammer and spoke the words of Tyr's holy turning!
. . . Nothin'. At all. And Sasha saw.
We ran.
And we've been found out. . . . I'm found out. I'm just a worthless chum-robbing thief.

Squirladax

Unslacken your packs on your backs! Time has come to flee this realm! Chahd the Betrayer has found us, and in blind, shrieking panic born anew, I must lead my band madly spilling through a desperate choosing of doors.

SENSATE PALATE CLEANSER

MAKES ABOUT 2 QUARTS

1 tablespoon unsalted butter

1 medium leek (white and light green parts), chopped

Kosher salt

3 medium-small English cucumbers

3 cups low-sodium chicken broth

⅔ cup half-and-half

1½ tablespoons fresh lemon juice

Freshly ground black pepper

3 tablespoons snipped fresh chives

The appetite of the Society of Sensation knows no bounds: they are the ultimate explorers of experience, which takes them to the extremes of the palate. But the unfamiliar can only really be tasted against the baseline of the common. The Sensates lighted on the free cucumber soup that came with a cheap inn room at the Slumbering Lamb in Sigil as the perfect neutral reference points for embarking on a culinary adventure. Area taverns catering to this clientele turned this dish into a chilled leek-and-cucumber-based puree. Even for those without the restless curiosity of a Sensate, this smooth and mild soup is a refreshing appetizer no matter where it's consumed.

In a small saucepan over medium-high heat, melt the butter. Add the leek and ½ teaspoon salt and cook, stirring, until the leek begins to soften, about 2½ minutes. Adjust the heat to medium-low, cover, and continue cooking, stirring occasionally, until the leek has released its juices, about 5 minutes longer. Remove from the heat and let cool briefly.

Meanwhile, peel one of the cucumbers, leaving about one-fourth of the skin on for a little texture and color. Peel the other two cucumbers completely. Halve all the cucumbers lengthwise and remove the seeds. Finely dice one of the fully peeled halves and set aside. Cut the remaining five halves into roughly 1-inch pieces.

In a blender, combine one-third of the roughly chopped cucumbers, one-third of the leek, and 1 cup of the chicken broth and puree until very smooth, about 40 seconds. Pour the mixture into a large bowl (preferably stainless steel) and set aside. Repeat to blend another third of the cucumbers, leeks, and broth, pouring this batch into the bowl with the first one. For the last batch, combine the remaining roughly chopped cucumber, remaining leeks, and remaining 1 cup chicken broth in the blender; add the half-and-half; and puree. Add to the bowl, stir in the lemon juice and ¾ teaspoon salt, and season with pepper. Stir in the diced cucumber. Cover and refrigerate until cold, about 4 hours.

When ready to serve, stir the soup to blend again, and adjust the seasoning with additional salt and pepper, if necessary. Ladle into individual bowls and garnish each with a sprinkle of pepper and some chives.

FRIED BREAD AND SPICES

MAKES 6 SLICES

2½ teaspoons paprika

1 teaspoon ground cumin

1 teaspoon ground coriander

1 teaspoon ground fennel

1 teaspoon kosher salt

½ teaspoon freshly ground
black pepper

¼ teaspoon cayenne pepper

6 slices country, French, or
Italian bread, ¾ inch thick and
about 5 inches wide

½ cup extra-virgin olive oil

1 garlic clove (optional)

Some believe that everything is better fried. Whether or not you agree, you wouldn't want to miss out on Fried Bread and Spices available at most taverns in the Lower Ward of Sigil. A popular breakfast staple on the planets Oerth, Toril, and Krynn, it is often served with poached eggs. The version most common in the City of Doors includes a unique seasoning mixture that borrows from all of them, with hints of cumin, coriander, cayenne, and even fennel. Whatever is in it, it's sure to brighten your meal, your day, and your journey onto the next plane.

In a small bowl, combine the paprika, cumin, coriander, fennel, salt, black pepper, and cayenne and stir to incorporate. Brush both sides of each bread slice with about 2 teaspoons of the olive oil.

In a large nonstick skillet over medium heat, place as many slices of bread as will fit in a single layer. Cook, undisturbed, until golden brown on the bottom, about 5 minutes. Near the end of that time, sprinkle about 1 teaspoon of the spice mixture evenly over each slice of bread. Carefully flip the bread so the spiced side is down and continue to cook until lightly browned on the second side and fragrant, about 1½ minutes longer. Remove the bread from the pan, and repeat to cook the remaining slices. Rub each slice lightly on either side with the garlic clove, if desired, before serving.

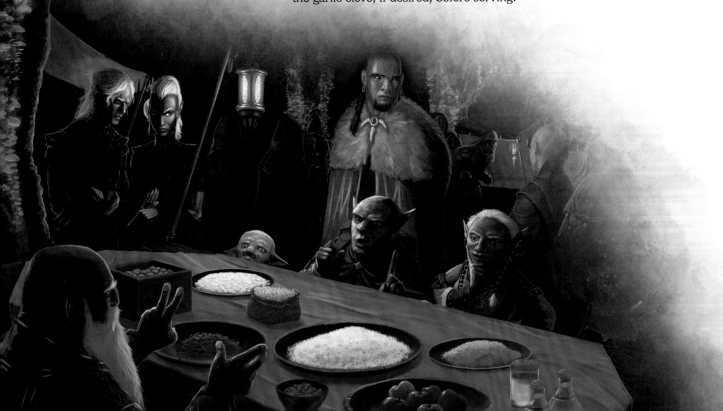

Beer Bread

MAKES ONE 9-INCH LOAF

3 cups all-purpose flour

1½ tablespoons granulated sugar

1 tablespoon baking powder

1 teaspoon kosher salt

½ teaspoon freshly ground black pepper

One 12-ounce bottle ale (preferably an IPA), or another style of beer (see Cook's Note)

3 tablespoons unsalted butter, melted

COOK'S NOTES

Different types of beer produce different flavors in this bread. For instance, India pale ale (IPA) provides a noticeably pleasant beer flavor, whereas American-style lagers are so mild they can be difficult to detect. Dark beers such as porter or stout provide a richer flavor along with a bit of residual bitterness.

Beer bread is sensational with soups, as a snack on its own, or as a sponge to soak up the gravied jus of roasted game. Just don't expect it to last long once it's out of the oven.

Many eateries across the multiverse claim to have the best beer-bread recipe, but Fortune's Wheel, an upscale canteen in Sigil's aristocratic Lady's Ward, really does. Any bread with beer in the dough is considered a beer bread, and the results are usually as middling as the common brew. However, this recipe from Fortune's Wheel yields a moist and chewy loaf that is bound to become a mealtime staple on any dinner table. Different types of beer yield distinctive flavors of bread and, depending on the varietal, it may even add leavening to the baking process, changing the ultimate density of the loaf. But regardless of the beer you choose (the Fortune's Wheel uses a dark, dry stout), it's all about the quality of the batter.

With a rack in the middle position, preheat the oven to 375°F. Coat a 9 by 5-inch loaf pan with nonstick cooking spray and set aside.

In a medium bowl, combine the flour, sugar, baking powder, salt, and pepper and whisk to incorporate. Add the beer and, using a flexible spatula, stir to form a lumpy batter (do not overmix). Pour the batter into the prepared pan and spread it into the corners, if necessary. Pour about 2 tablespoons of the melted butter evenly over the batter.

Bake the bread until deep golden brown and a skewer inserted in the center of the loaf comes out clean, about 55 minutes, rotating the pan and brushing the top of the loaf with the remaining 1 tablespoon butter halfway through. Transfer the pan to a wire rack and let cool for about 10 minutes. Remove the loaf from the pan, and let cool on the rack for 20 minutes longer. Slice the bread with a serrated knife and serve barely warm or at room temperature.

BACON-WRAPPED SMOKED MUSSELS

SERVES 4 AS A SNACK

6 slices bacon

24 highest-quality smoked mussels (see Cook's Note)

Sigil's lively marketplaces are brimming with strange, fresh meats and fish imported from across the greater multiverse. These expansive emporiums are an overwhelming explosion of scents, textures, colors, and flavors, not only making them a chef's dream but a breeding ground for new culinary ideas. Bacon-Wrapped Smoked Mussels is one such intrinsically Sigil meal on offer in many of the city's six wards. While the combination of pork and mollusk might seem unusual, this atypical culinary marriage is what makes the meal uniquely Sigil. An inspired combination of surf and turf, this dish has made its way across the multiverse as far as the Cutlass of Luskan on Toril, where fresh mussels are harvested in droves from the Sea of Swords, while the cured bacon is brought in almost daily from Mirabar via the River Mirar.

With a rack in the middle position, preheat the oven to 400°F. Line a plate with paper towels and set aside. Place a wire rack on a rimmed baking sheet and set aside.

In a medium nonstick skillet over medium-low heat, cook the bacon until it begins to render some fat, is softened, and is half cooked, about 8 minutes, flipping the pieces halfway through. Transfer the bacon to the prepared plate to drain briefly.

Move the bacon to a cutting board, setting the plate aside. Cut the slices in half crosswise. Lay two mussels on a half slice of bacon, wrap the bacon around them, and secure with a toothpick. Repeat with the remaining mussels and bacon. Arrange the bundles on the prepared wire rack about 1 inch apart.

Place the baking sheet in the oven and roast the mussels until browned and starting to crisp, about 8 minutes. Transfer to the plate and let rest for 1 minute. Serve immediately; these should be eaten hot and fresh.

COOK'S NOTE

Plump, high-quality mussels are imperative here—it's not worth making the recipe with tinned smoked mussels. Source the mussels from a small producer such as Ducktrap River of Maine, a smokehouse, or a fishmonger that sells smoked fish.

CHICKPEA AND SPICY SAUSAGE SOUP

MAKES ABOUT 2½ QUARTS

Three 15-ounce cans chickpeas

¼ cup extra-virgin olive oil

¾ pound chouriço, linguiça, or Spanish (dry-cured) chorizo, halved lengthwise and sliced ½ inch thick (see Cook's Note)

1 large yellow onion, chopped

2 large celery ribs, trimmed and sliced ½ inch thick

2 large bay leaves

Kosher salt

1 tablespoon pressed or grated garlic

½ teaspoon red pepper flakes

4 cups low-sodium chicken broth

1 cup water

One 8-ounce can tomato sauce

Freshly ground black pepper

⅓ cup chopped fresh parsley

COOK'S NOTES

If you like spicy heat, consider choosing hot chouriço.

To make it a meal, serve the soup over hot, freshly cooked rice.

Serving equally well as a solo course or as a starter paired with a lighter main, Chickpea and Spicy Sausage Soup is a hearty, delicious, protein-filled potage. As served in Sigil, this soup incorporates Sweet Larissa's sausages, imported from Plague-Mort—the less you know about how she makes them the better. But one thing you will know is she makes them hot: with the sort of spices mortals should avoid unless in ethereal form. The chickpeas offer a starchy and earthy sanctuary from the oily, spicy sausage and red pepper flakes, all of it swimming in a garlicky chicken broth, flavored with tomato. Common variations on this dish introduce tarragon for a pungent and inspired twist on the classic. Although widely available, and often considered a meal for the masses, this is nonetheless a delectable soup that has rightfully earned its place in the heart of many citizens of the greater multiverse.

Line a plate with paper towels and set aside. Empty two cans of the chickpeas, with their liquid, into a medium bowl. Drain the third can, rinse the chickpeas, and transfer to the same bowl. Set aside.

In a large saucepan or Dutch oven over medium heat, warm the olive oil until shimmering. Add the chouriço and cook until it browns slightly and tints the oil red, 5 to 6 minutes, stirring once or twice. With a slotted spoon, transfer the sausage to the prepared plate to drain. Pour all but about 1 tablespoon of the oil into a small bowl, and set aside.

Return the pan to medium heat and add the onion, celery, bay leaves, and ½ teaspoon salt. Cook, stirring, until the vegetables begin to soften, about 3 minutes. Adjust the heat to medium-low, cover, and continue cooking, stirring occasionally, until the vegetables have released their juices, about 4 minutes longer. Add the garlic and red pepper flakes and cook, stirring, until fragrant, about 40 seconds. Add the chicken broth, water, tomato sauce, and chickpeas with their liquid. Adjust the heat to medium-high and bring to a boil. Adjust the heat to low, cover, and let simmer to soften the chickpeas further and blend the flavors, stirring occasionally, about 40 minutes. Add the cooked sausage and 1 teaspoon salt, season with black pepper, and continue simmering to heat the sausage through. Remove the bay leaves, add most of the parsley, and stir to mix. Adjust the seasoning with additional salt and black pepper, if necessary. Divide among individual plates. Drizzle with the reserved sausage cooking oil and sprinkle with some of the remaining parsley before serving.

Fire-Wrapped Golden Fish

SERVES 4

6 cups canola oil or corn oil

Kosher salt

2 teaspoons freshly ground
black pepper

1½ teaspoons cayenne pepper

Ice cubes

About 1½ cups cold tap water

1 cup all-purpose flour

1½ tablespoons chili powder

2 teaspoons garlic powder

1½ pounds firm, meaty white-fleshed
fish fillets (such as halibut, tilapia,
or mahi-mahi), skinned and cut into
3 by 1-inch strips

¾ cup plus 1 tablespoon cold
sparkling water

Lime wedges for serving

While Sigil's Great Bazaar is perhaps the most famous market in the known multiverse—a vibrant conflux of cultures and cuisines—this self-proclaimed "city at the center of the multiverse" also boasts countless storefronts and street bazaars, offering equally rare and exciting gastronomy. Fire-Wrapped Golden Fish is one such inexpensive delicacy, readily acquired in the Lower Ward or the more destitute Hive Ward. As quick to fry as it is to consume, this chili-and-cayenne-tinged, batter-fried white fish is a feast for the taste buds. Best served sizzling-hot, straight from the pan, wrapped in locally cultivated lettuce or a flatbread for easy ingestion en route to the next plane.

Preheat the oven to 200°F. Line a large rimmed baking sheet with a double layer of paper towels and set aside. Place a wire rack on another large rimmed baking sheet and set aside.

Clip a deep-fry or candy thermometer to the side of a medium Dutch oven over medium-high heat and warm the canola oil to 360°F. In a small bowl, combine 2 teaspoons salt, the black pepper, and ¾ teaspoon of the cayenne and stir to mix.

While the oil heats, fill a large bowl one-third of the way with ice and add the tap water. In a medium bowl (preferably stainless steel), combine the flour, chili powder, garlic powder, remaining ¾ teaspoon cayenne, and ¾ teaspoon salt and whisk to incorporate. Set this bowl in the bowl of ice water to chill the flour mixture.

Spread the fish on a platter or a third rimmed baking sheet. Sprinkle the fish all over with the seasoning mixture and set aside.

When the oil is at temperature, add the sparkling water to the flour mixture and stir just until the wet and dry ingredients are mixed but still a little lumpy (do not overmix).

Add six pieces of fish to the batter and coat them thoroughly. Using tongs or chopsticks, remove three pieces, allowing excess batter to drip back into the bowl, and slip the fish into the oil. Wait 30 seconds and repeat with the other three battered pieces. Fry until slightly puffed and golden brown, turning the pieces once or twice to promote even frying and prevent them from sticking to each other, adjusting the heat as necessary to maintain 360°F, 4 to 5 minutes. Using a spider skimmer, slotted spoon, or long tongs, transfer the fried fish to the paper towel–lined baking sheet to drain for about 30 seconds. Sprinkle the fried fish lightly with salt, transfer to the prepared wire rack set, and place in the oven to keep warm. Allow the oil to return to 360°F and repeat until all the fish are cooked. Serve immediately with lime wedges.

EMERALD CHICKEN

SERVES 4 TO 6

8 ounces chicken livers, trimmed of fat, membranes, and connective tissue

Kosher salt and freshly ground black pepper

4 split bone-in chicken breasts (10 to 12 ounces each)

2 tablespoons neutral oil

1 pound tomatillos, husked and washed

3 medium yellow onions; 1 thickly sliced and 2 quartered

6 garlic cloves; 3 left whole with skins on and 3 pressed or grated

3 medium serrano or jalapeño chiles (see Cook's Note)

⅓ cup chopped fresh cilantro leaves and small stems

2 teaspoons fresh lime juice

1 teaspoon granulated sugar

1 pound baby spinach

COOK'S NOTES

The heat of serranos and jalapeños can vary significantly, so you may want to take a tiny nibble to gauge how hot yours are and use more than three if it seems too tame. Here, we use them whole, with their seeds and inner membranes, to harness all the heat.

The chicken livers can pop and spit a bit as they cook, so if you have a splatter screen, this is a great time to deploy it.

Rice or quinoa make good accompaniments.

It is fact that the only way in or out of Sigil is through one of the city's innumerable portals. It is also fact that while in Sigil, one *must* try the famous Emerald Chicken. Gifted its name from the splash of chopped greens, intermingled with chunks of fowl, chicken livers, onions, and a strong dash of incendiary spices, Emerald Chicken demands an adventurous palate— it was originally made for tieflings with fiendspices—and a cool glass of ale to quench the burn. A milder version became famous in far-off Purskul, on Toril, in eateries such as the Owlroost Head.

Rinse the chicken livers, pat dry with paper towels, and put in the refrigerator.

In a small bowl or ramekin, combine 2½ teaspoons salt and 1 teaspoon pepper, stir to mix, and set aside. Working with one chicken breast at a time, gently shimmy your finger between the skin and the meat, loosening but not detaching the skin. Fold over the skin to expose the meat, sprinkle about one-fourth of the salt and pepper mixture evenly over the meat, and lay the skin back in place. Repeat with the remaining chicken breasts and salt and pepper. Put the chicken in the refrigerator.

With a rack in the middle position, preheat the oven to 325°F.

In a large ovenproof skillet over high heat, warm 2 teaspoons of the neutral oil until shimmering. Add the tomatillos, sliced onion, whole garlic, and chiles and cook, undisturbed, until deeply charred on the bottom, about 6 minutes. Using tongs, flip everything and cook, undisturbed, until the second side is charred, about 6 minutes longer. Transfer the tomatillos, onion, and chiles to a blender. Transfer the garlic to a small plate. When the garlic is cool enough to handle, squeeze the cloves out of the skins and add to the blender along with the cilantro, lime juice, sugar, and 1 teaspoon salt. Blend until the mixture is thoroughly pureed. Adjust the seasoning with additional salt, if necessary, and blend into a salsa.

Set the skillet over medium-high heat, add 2 teaspoons neutral oil, and warm until shimmering. Add the chicken, skin-side down, and cook, undisturbed, until well browned, 3 to 4 minutes. Flip the chicken pieces and tuck the onion quarters around the chicken. Transfer the skillet to the oven and roast the chicken until it registers 160°F on an instant-read thermometer, 25 to 40 minutes. Leaving the onions and chicken juices in the skillet, transfer the chicken to a plate and let rest for 5 minutes. Cut each chicken breast in half crosswise and cover with foil to keep warm. CONTINUED ➜

EMERALD CHICKEN CONTINUED

While the chicken rests, set a strainer over a medium bowl.

In a large nonstick skillet over medium-high heat, warm about 1 tablespoon of the chicken juices. Add as much spinach as will fit comfortably in the skillet and cook, stirring and turning constantly, until wilted and bright green, about 1 minute. Add the remaining spinach in batches, cooking and stirring, until all the spinach is wilted and bright green, about 3 minutes longer. About halfway through the cooking time, add the pressed garlic. Scrape the spinach and garlic into the strainer and, using tongs, squeeze to release as much liquid as possible. Add the drained spinach to the pan with the onions and chicken juices, add ½ teaspoon salt and ½ teaspoon pepper, and toss to coat. Arrange the spinach, onions, and chicken on a serving platter, and set aside.

Return the nonstick skillet to medium-high heat, add the remaining 2 teaspoons neutral oil, and warm until shimmering. Lightly sprinkle the chicken livers all over with salt and pepper and cook, undisturbed, until the bottoms are lightly browned, about 2½ minutes. Flip the livers and cook until the second sides are lightly browned, about 2 minutes longer (do not overcook—they should remain rosy inside). Using tongs, remove the livers from the pan and arrange on the platter with the spinach and chicken.

Pour about half the salsa over the chicken and livers. Serve immediately, passing the remaining salsa on the side.

HARMONIOUS BARRACKS MEATLOAF

SERVES 6 TO 8

2 cups lightly packed, torn crustless pieces French, Italian, or other sturdy white bread (1-inch pieces)

⅔ cup whole or 2% milk

2 eggs, beaten

1 tablespoon extra-virgin olive oil

1 medium yellow onion, finely chopped

Kosher salt

2 tablespoons pressed or grated garlic

2 tablespoons finely chopped fresh rosemary

1 tablespoon chopped fresh thyme

1½ pounds ground lamb

½ pound ground chuck (preferably 85% lean)

1 teaspoon freshly ground black pepper

½ cup finely chopped fresh parsley

If you intend to police the chaotic streets of Sigil, it's best not to do it on an empty stomach. The warriors of the Harmonium are deeply dedicated to keeping order but are perhaps not so adventuresome in their tastes, so this rich, filling meal-in-itself will keep a soldier on the march for hours on end. Heaps of it are hot and plentiful in their barracks in the Lady's Ward. To maximize its proteins, this dish includes not just lamb but a medley of meats, which gives it its distinctive, hearty flavor. Ironically, a certain quantity of this meatloaf somehow finds its way into the hands of street vendors—this is, after all, a town where everyone finds a way to turn a quick profit.

With a rack in the middle position, preheat the oven to 375°F. Line a rimmed baking sheet with aluminum foil. Line a large wire rack with foil and poke holes in the foil. Set the rack on the baking sheet and set aside.

In a large bowl, combine the bread and milk and let soak, stirring occasionally, until softened, about 15 minutes. With a potato masher or fork, mash the mixture to a loose paste. Add the eggs and stir vigorously to combine.

In a medium skillet over medium heat, warm the olive oil until shimmering. Add the onion and ½ teaspoon salt and cook, stirring, until softened, about 4 minutes. Add the garlic, rosemary, and thyme and continue to cook, stirring, until fragrant, about 40 seconds. Scrape into a bowl and let cool to room temperature.

Add the lamb, chuck, onion mixture, 2 teaspoons salt, and the pepper to the bread mixture. Set aside 1 tablespoon of the parsley, and add the remaining 7 tablespoons to the bowl. Fold and stir the mixture gently until well blended. On the prepared rack, form the mixture into a roughly 9 by 5-inch loaf.

Bake the meatloaf until an instant-read thermometer inserted near the center registers 155° to 160°F, about 1¼ hours. Let the meatloaf cool for about 10 minutes, then transfer to a cutting board or serving plate. Slice it with a serrated blade and serve.

CHIRPER'S SUGAR BISCUITS

MAKES 12 BUNS

¼ cup granulated sugar

1 tablespoon finely grated lemon zest

3 tablespoons packed light or dark brown sugar

¾ teaspoon ground cinnamon

½ teaspoon ground cardamom

1 pinch kosher salt

1 sheet frozen all-butter puff pastry (see Cook's Notes), thawed according to package directions and still cool

2 tablespoons unsalted butter, at room temperature, plus 2 tablespoons melted

COOK'S NOTES

The dimensions of puff pastry sheets vary by brand, so depending on which one you use, you may or may not have to roll it to the required length. Regardless, make sure your pastry is completely thawed, so you can unfold it initially, and roll it up with the filling, without it cracking. It should still be cool, though, because warm puff pastry can become sticky. Finally, don't allow the baked buns to cool completely in the muffin tin, or they will stick to the cups.

All that said, don't allow all this information daunt you. The buns are, in fact, easy to form and bake, and easier yet to eat. On that note, they're best within a couple of hours of baking. You can, however, re-crisp them with about a 5-minute stay in a 350°F oven.

No matter what you order at Chirper's in the Market Ward of Sigil—from the Niflheim stag ribs to the slaad legs—the sugar biscuits are a complimentary finale. Whether you came for the dancing, the Seawind theater, an art exhibition, or just a quick visit to gawk at the Skull Museum, it is always worth grabbing a bite at Chirper's for the dessert alone. Acquiring the Bytopian chestnuts required to make the puffy dough might require planar travel, but primes can approximate the right taste by adding some cinnamon and cardamom to the mix. Best served with honey as a dip for an extra dash of decadence.

In a medium bowl, combine 2 tablespoons of the granulated sugar and the lemon zest and stir until the sugar is moist and fragrant. Add the brown sugar, cinnamon, cardamom, and salt and stir to mix thoroughly. Set aside 2 tablespoons of the mixture.

Place a sheet of parchment paper on your work surface and evenly sprinkle the remaining 2 tablespoons granulated sugar over it. On the sugared paper, unfold the puff pastry (which should be rectangular) and, if it is less than 15 inches long, place a second parchment sheet over it and use a rolling pin to gently roll it to that length (taking care not to press too hard, which compresses the layers, decreasing their puff when baked). Remove the top parchment sheet. If necessary, using your fingers, gently loosen the long edge of the pastry nearest you from the bottom piece of parchment paper (this will make it easier to begin rolling it with the filling). Evenly spread the room-temperature butter over the pastry and sprinkle the larger quantity of the sugar mixture over the butter, all the way to the edges. Lay a piece of parchment paper over the sugar mixture, gently press down to help the mixture adhere, and remove the parchment.

Starting with the long side that you loosened, gently roll the pastry into a very tight, even, compact cylinder. Pinch the seam along the entire length of the cylinder to seal (it may pop open as the buns bake, which is fine). Slide the cylinder and the parchment sheet it's on onto a large baking sheet, cover with plastic wrap, and refrigerate until firm, about 45 minutes.

With a rack in the middle position, preheat the oven to 400°F. Coat the cups of a standard muffin tin with nonstick cooking spray, and set aside.

Remove the plastic from the pastry, place the cylinder seam-side down on a cutting board, and, using a serrated knife in a sawing motion,

CONTINUED →

174   FLAVORS OF THE MULTIVERSE

CHIRPER'S SUGAR BISCUITS CONTINUED

cut the cylinder in half crosswise. Cut each half into sixths and place, cut-side up, in a prepared muffin cup.

Bake the buns until puffed and dark golden brown, about 20 minutes, rotating the muffin tin about halfway through. Remove the buns from the oven and, working quickly, brush with the melted butter and sprinkle each with about ½ teaspoon of the reserved sugar mixture. Let cool for 3 minutes, then carefully remove the buns from the muffin tin while still hot. Let cool on the rack to room temperature (they'll crisp up more as they cool) before serving.

SILVERFRUIT PIE

SERVES 8

2 teaspoons unsalted butter, at room temperature, plus 5 tablespoons melted and still warm

14 whole graham crackers, broken into rough pieces

3 tablespoons light brown sugar

Kosher salt

One 20-ounce can lychees (peeled, pitted, and in heavy syrup)

12 ounces mascarpone, at cool room temperature

3 tablespoons confectioners' sugar

2 teaspoons rosewater

1 teaspoon vanilla extract

2 tablespoons apple jelly

1½ teaspoons finely grated lemon zest

COOK'S NOTES

Rather than warming the apple jelly on the stovetop, you can warm it in a microwave-safe container in the microwave, using partial power, for about 30 seconds, stopping to check and stir it about every 10 seconds.

Even though you drain and dry the lychees, they'll retain enough moisture to weep on the pie if they sit for too long. It's best to serve the pie no more than an hour after glazing it. If you have leftovers, refrigerate them and expect the jam to slide off the lychees and pool between them and at the edges of the crust. If you'd like, use a small bit of paper towel to blot away visible liquid before serving.

Let it be known, silverfruit, also known as lychee or soapberry, makes for a truly heavenly pie. This medium-size, pink-skinned berry is known for being especially crisp and juicy, with hints of citrus and a floral aroma. But as a pie filling it's surprisingly creamy and custard-like, and it pairs wonderfully with a toasted, flaky crust. The Golden Bariaur Inn (in Sigil's Lady's Ward), which caters to highfalutin clientele from the Upper Planes, serves an astoundingly good slice of this silky dessert. Since Sigil has no natural resources, silverfruit is one of the many uniquely curated imports from the vast array of worlds to which the greater metropolis provides access.

With a rack in the middle position, preheat the oven to 350°F. Coat a 9-inch pie plate with the room-temperature butter, and set aside.

In a food processor, process the graham crackers to fine crumbs, about 20 seconds. Add the brown sugar and 1 pinch salt and pulse to combine. With the motor running, slowly add the melted butter through the feed tube and process until the mixture resembles wet sand, about 20 seconds. Pour the mixture into the pie plate and press into an even, compact layer across the bottom and up the sides. Wipe out the food processor work bowl to use again.

Bake the crust until lightly browned and fragrant, about 12 minutes, rotating the pie plate about halfway through. Transfer to a wire rack and let cool to room temperature (the crust will firm up as it cools).

Meanwhile, drain the lychees well and blot them dry with paper towel. Line a plate or baking sheet with paper towels in a double layer. Cut each lychee in half, place them cut sides down on the paper towel–lined plate, and refrigerate until needed, at least 1 hour.

Add the mascarpone, confectioners' sugar, rosewater, vanilla, and ¼ teaspoon salt to the food processor and pulse until combined and smooth, stopping once or twice to scrape down the work bowl, about 10 two-second pulses. Scrape the mixture into the crust, gently spread it in an even layer, and refrigerate until firmer, at least 1 hour. Arrange the lychees, cut-sides down, over the mascarpone, covering the entire surface, and gently press them into the mixture to anchor.

In a small saucepan over medium heat, warm the apple jelly until warm to the touch and beginning to become fluid, stirring to smooth out any lumps. Off heat, cool the fluid jelly for about 5 minutes. Stir it again and, using a pastry brush, gently dab and brush the jelly over the lychees. Refrigerate for 30 minutes, sprinkle the lemon zest over the pie, and serve immediately.

KAETH

MAKES ABOUT 2½ CUPS

⅓ cup ground dark-roast coffee

3 cups water

2 tablespoons light brown sugar

½ teaspoon molasses (not blackstrap)

1 cinnamon stick, broken in half

1 teaspoon crushed anise seeds

1½ tablespoons finely grated orange zest

1 small pinch kosher salt

COOK'S NOTE

If you prefer your kaeth iced, pour it from the French press into a jar with a tight-fitting lid. Allow it to cool to room temperature, seal the lid, and refrigerate until cold, about 3 hours. Serve over ice.

Kaeth, or coffee, is an aromatic brew made from ground roasted beans and is famous for its invigorating properties, making it a prevalent day starter throughout the worlds of the multiverse. In Sigil, the City of Doors, planar sightseers can sample from a wide array of coffee beans and beverages from countless planets. Kaeth, as it is commonly called on the planet Toril, has developed into quite the delicacy along the Sword Coast, where it is now imported in droves. In the nation of Sembia, a popular method of preparation features a blend of melted chocolate and liquor. In some areas, kaeth is so popular that it has become more profitable than the tea trade. The peoples of the planet Krynn drink tarbean tea and kefre, both of which are derived from vibrant, dark-roasted beans and frequently served black. In contrast, citizens of the Outer Planes imbibe numerous spiced and creamed variants of kaeth, including the notable Mountain Majesty of Mount Celestia. On the planet Oerth, coffee trends more acidic and is frequently blended into creamy liquors to grant an extra kick. But perhaps the most notable, kav'la, in which creamed coconut milk is swirled into a malted, dark, nutty roast, is served in tall, ornate ceramic vessels and is easily found in the cultured bazaars of Sigil. Regardless of which varietal you choose, kaeth, in its endless forms, serves as a caffeine-infused pick-me-up, whether on the trail or in the safe confines of one's homestead.

Place the coffee in a French press and set aside.

In a medium saucepan over medium-high heat, combine the water, brown sugar, molasses, cinnamon stick, anise seeds, orange zest, and salt and bring to a boil, stirring to dissolve the sugar. Adjust the heat to medium and let simmer until the mixture is fragrant and reduced to about 2⅔ cups, about 14 minutes. Pour the mixture into the French press and stir to fully moisten the coffee grounds. Position the lid on the pot and let steep for 4 minutes before slowly pressing the plunger. Serve immediately.

THE FEYWILD

TIME TO MAKE A STAND! Utilizing the astral gateways of Sigil, and pursued by CHAHD'S SKELETAL HORDES, our heroes retreat to THE FEYWILD to finally confront the villainous VAMPEER!

Squirladax
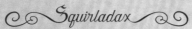

If only a proper plan might spring from mine head-guts! Fleeing this City of Doors in terror-stricken cowardice, we spring forth through the door once, only to spring backwards twice! A sandy hellscape! Door! A kingdom under the sea! And but always one door behind us, slender, pallid, skinless fiends sneering their death-mask smirks that nearly cry out from lipless teeth, "We know your idiocy!"

Skeletons. With their diabolical sarcastic grins! And always, a velveteen capèd incubus with pasted yellow hair. Chahd, the Betrayer. Vampyr. Zounds! We must find a place to hide!

Alas, my senses are assailed by cheery, cherry mists, flitting faerie feathers, and sweet winds that do breeze from welcoming vanilla skies. I have found the place I seek, and hence proclaimed unto my charge:

"Friends! Behold the Feywild! Brightest twin to darkest Shadowfell. 'Tis here that Chahd and his undead minions will be weakest. 'Tis here, we will make our final stand."

Bri'An
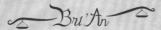

Tyr protect our flight, for in twinkling twilight, Dint's stubby, creaking legs lose pace with us. And as I fall back to assist, I fall back into shifty old Bri'An. True Bri'An, the one who wonders to himself why he bothers to talk this crappy, pious cleric talk. The one who notices the others are several paces ahead. The one who should break open Dint's bronze paunch, steal back his jewels, and be off before all is dead. And yet I don't do it.

Dint snorts unhappily.

Dint

My clockwork ticks with the tockings of bitterness. As I am not designed to resolve gnomish emotions, I find this tocking distressing.

My business is ruined. My ticks and tocks want only of return . . . to my ruined spellship Dashor.

Deelia
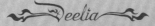

Morning comes, and I sup upon Seelie Court Cheese and Potato Soup from this nameless eladrin inn we have sheltered in. The others are mortuarily quiet. I find my ears longing for the blubbering prattle that regularly sparks my contempt.

Gaze I now through the window at a nearby hill, the ruined stump of an elven guard tower atop its peak. I think mournfully of Shadow's Edge.

I have been to the afterlife, the Queen's Shadowfell, and this I know now to be a defect of that sublimely dreary place. Ne'er did I see a proper roadhouse! A place of feastings and . . . I don't know . . . dancing and merriment . . . for the Shadowfell I visited 'tis kind of a dump.

Roadhouse, yes. You are the peace that could be born of a Shadow's Edge Cheflord.

Of which I am not.

Soon, Chahd's icy fingers will surely choke these warm thoughts from my soul.

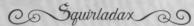

Squirladax

WOULD MY LIFE A BOOK, ALL CHAPTERS 'ERE BE NAMÈD "BETRAYED!" For it turns out that Bri'An 'twere NEVER ANY CLERIC OF TYR! Thief and scoundrel, patriarch of lies! Yet, even now, HE plays the card of SUFFERER, with weeping quiver upon the plates of his lying mouth-hole!

From Sasha's eyes came a waterfall of tears, slipping her leech children off their ancestral cheek. She looked down yet always up to the stocky false Bri'An!

OH, 'TIS GETS WORSE!

For even as I write this, DINT now chimes with a glockenspiel of disloyalty!

TAKE THIS I CANNOT!

Deelia

EVERYTHING GOES TO HELLS! Squirladax litigates a case for solidarity, but without his powdered mop-wig, the poor goblin's legal authority is robbed of him! As Bri'An's confessions of faithlessness slip a dagger into our ribs, the Otter Gnome slits our throats with a clanging RESIGNATION OF MEMBERSHIP from our Dark Tables!

In a mighty roar that scattered Baked Goat Cheese upon the inn's polished floors, Squirladax howled thusly, "Returned thee, I see, to your Arch-Nemesis ways, have you?!"

Dint choked dispassionately, "Death is certain for this Bureau. No logic nor assistance can I grant. I will return to Dashor now."

"And what of precious, sparkling Diamonds?" wheezed Squirladax

Dint puffed, "There are no Diamonds."

A shock befell all.

Kettled rage boiled in Squirladax, "KEEP YOUR DIAMONDS, MASTER OF TREASON! I will have no more sight of you!" And Squirladax fled to the outhouse to mourn.

A quiet sadness. Bri'An, his scales soggy, fell to the bench.

Then Sasha, ashen and saddest of all, laid buttery hand to Dint's bronze pauldron.

Whispered she, "You only ever helped us, and as you return to your home, the lands where Otters and Gnomes live in harmony, know that, for you, there will always be treason in my heart."

Dint is gone.

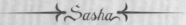

Sasha

Chahd is coming. Squirladax has not left the outhouse since yesterday. Deelia's been downing bottles of Saerloonian Glowfire at the inn. As I wander the grounds near the hill, I see Bri'An in the ruined tower gazing afar.

If Squirladax believes Dint is junk and Bri'An is garbage, then what am I? I am a fraud. Just like Bri'An. I've read *Volo's Guide* so hard . . . sauced my limbs, bled myself dizzy, expanded my breath bellows to near popping, and raised a colony of leeches on my face . . . but I am no closer to becoming the warrior Squirladax needs.

His gift of that book was wasted on me. I've failed my party. Again.

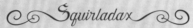

Squirladax

This house of out reminds me of the Caves of Calmness.

Pronounced strangely by not-goblins, the Caves were a soothing grotto of the mirthiest, most charitable goblinfolk one could ever randomly encounter.

Raided we were, often, by bullying humanfolk, twisting my heart sour. Took they from us our treasures, not just of coin, but those of pride and stout-heartedness. Now I steal these treasures back, but from mine own minions . . . nay! My friends.

Dint was right to leave.

What's this I hear?

"OHMUHGAHD!!!!!! UHHHHH MUHHHHHH GAAAAHHHHHHHHH!!!!!!"

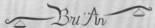

Bri'An

Spotted the skeletal bastards from the ruined tower, I did, and then calmly called out, "Gods! They come!" or something to that effect.

Tyr then did grant my stubby limbs much speed and . . . nah he didn't.

Suck I.

Wait. . . . A goblin-man comes to rush me, his arms outstretched. . . .

Deelia

WILL WE DIE? For certain! But punch we first?! NINE HELLS YES we will, on Chahd's stupidest of faces! This is the song stirred in me by the words just spoken!

You see, sitting piggy about the back of Bri'An, Squirladax called UNTO US in a voice more powerful than ten irritating goblins!

"Forces of the dreaded Shadowfell, prepare to march on this realm!"

Sad Sasha was the first to answer: "But we have no front line! No adequate fighter!"

OH QUEEN, tell no one that I was actually impressed when hated goblinman turned his beady eyes unto our forlorn hearts and pronounced with shrill grandeur.

"Sasha! The mutilations you've inflicted upon thyself are greater than any wound of death! Thus, you are the mightiest WARRIOR . . . in easily like three miles!"

Continued he, weaseling his logic upon our wills.

"DEELIA! Your Queen shall smile at your noble stand against Orcus's minions! And you, UNHOLY AVENGER, shall burn Chahd's bones as kindling!"

He then turned to the smallest dragon-man.

"Bri'An. Your faith may be a lie, but my faith in you is not. Take up Tyr's banner one last time, old friend."

TO WAR!

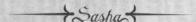

WARFARE GUYYYSSS! Let me catch you up! So, there's this old watchtower ruin thing on this hill. That's HOMEBASE. Two paths up the hill to the tower, one NORTH, one SOUTH. Chahd is coming from the NORTH, so Deelia has ordered that we pepper the north slope. . . . WITH TRAPS, GUYS! TRAPS! Tripwires! Crossbows! SPIKED PITS! ISN'T THAT WICKED?

The SOUTH slope is our escape route if things go sideways.

HERE'S THE PLAN!

The Bureau will stand upon the hill and "vex Chahd." Chahd, now "vexed," will surely release his skeletal minions charging up the hill . . . INTO THE TRAPS! THEN, we reveal our wrath, attacking viciously until we KILL us a FREAKING VAMPEER, which is, I guess, easier than killing a Vampire. . . .

But still, really cool!

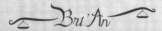

They come close, now, from the north. Some twenty strong . . . Against four.

Tyr, I've never prayed to you before. Grant me righteous speed as 'twere it likely that mine friends will be flayed screaming and suckled alive at the snapping smiles of Skeletal Vampeergroup.

A light rain now falls . . . which will only make my plated feet slippy.

Uh . . . thanks Tyr.

 Deelia

CHAHD AND HIS COLUMN OF DEATH HAVE ARRIVED!

I must now draw him to mine trappèd field! Let a DUELING OF VEXES COMMENCE!

Velveteen capèd Chahd, speaks with haughty loudness over the rains and spans betwixt us.

"Ah, the Tasty Tetrad! Even now, I sauce and season your cadavers in my mind's kitchen, to be prepared tenderly and servèd . . . to my master."

It is now, NOW that I unleash the vexing scornings of wit, "Never, betrayer! Bet I not that your master doesn't even dislike you!"

Paused, did Chahd, as my vexing does take hold! Clearèd his throat, he croaks, "Do you sayeth . . . wait. . . . You are saying he likes me? Or that he doesn't like me? Because I can assure you—"

"NO ONE LIKES YOU, CHAHD!," bellowed a presumptuous but not incorrect Sasha.

Worn plainly on his stupid face, a perfect vexing achieved, we hold as he will surely now unleash his minions unto the slaughtering of our many traps before us!

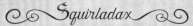 Squirladax

VEXÈD CHAHD does now **leisurely** lead his columns around from the north, circling our hill, and unto the SOUTH! The clear, trap-less passage to up here with us!

Calls Chahd out, "Do you think I STUPID? Only a Shadow's Edge **novice** could reveal her machinations so! Let me to the guessing! Traps? Worry not, I shall be with you soon enough."

All is lost, but for one last card in my Tarokka Deck. I shall weave inspiring bardic magic!

Sasha asks if she is to hold the front line, whilst Deelia lays about damaging spells, and to Bri'An the restoration of vigor!

Instead, I say:

"Remember, my friends.

There is truly only one rule in War!

GO OUT THERE . . .

. . . and just be yourself. Cuz that's . . . ya know . . . what they're looking for."

And I can feel their hearts swell with braveness.

Yet then, Chahd marches up from the south, and he did smile a wide toothèd grin, and by the GODS . . .

HE HAD FANGS!

ELVEN FLATBREAD

MAKES ONE 13 BY 9-INCH FOCACCIA

3 cups all-purpose flour or bread flour

1 packet (2¼ teaspoons) instant or Rapid Rise yeast

2 teaspoons kosher salt

1¾ cups lukewarm (105° to 115°F) water

5 tablespoons extra-virgin olive oil

1 tablespoon unsalted butter, at room temperature

Vegetables (such as halved cherry or grape tomatoes, sliced shallots or red onions, sliced mini bell peppers, and scallions)

Fresh herbs for garnish (such as parsley or basil sprigs)

Sliced black olives for garnish (optional)

Large-flake salt (such as Maldon)

Elven Flatbread is much more of a delight than its unassuming name suggests. A mosaic of colors and flavors, the thinly sliced vegetables, edible flora, and wild herbs are so elegantly placed atop this chewy focaccia that you *almost* want to admire it more than eat it. A cornucopia of garden-fresh components frequently make starring appearances—from onions, bell peppers, chives, and cherry tomatoes to sunflowers, elderflowers, squash blossoms, and sprigs of basil. Almost nothing is off-limits when it comes to topping; the only (unspoken) rule is to keep it vibrant and arrange them artfully. Despite elven flatbread being a "simple" bread recipe, Feywild eladrin pride themselves on flare and personal presentation. During harvest holidays, each flatbread is presented as a long and ornate loaf that serves as both a centerpiece and a meal starter for dipping in sharp, fragrant olive oils.

In a large bowl, combine the flour, yeast, and kosher salt and whisk to incorporate. Make a well in the center, add the water and, using a wooden spoon or your hands, stir around the perimeter of the well to incorporate the dry ingredients into the wet, creating a mass of sticky dough (it will look a little lumpy, which is fine). Pour 1½ teaspoons of the olive oil over the dough, and turn the dough to coat lightly. Cover the bowl and refrigerate until the dough has about doubled in bulk, at least 12 hours or up to 48 hours.

A couple of hours before you're ready to bake, coat a 13 by 9-inch baking dish with the butter and then with nonstick cooking spray. Add 2 tablespoons olive oil to the center of the dish and tilt to spread the oil. Pull the dough away from the sides of the bowl to deflate. Place in the prepared baking dish, roll in the oil to coat well, and re-shape it into a loose ball. Cover and let rest at room temperature until doubled in bulk, 2½ to 4 hours (timing will depend on the ambient temperature).

When ready to top and bake, with a rack in the middle position, preheat the oven to 425°F. Pour 2 tablespoons olive oil over the dough and spread evenly over the surface. Using your fingers, gently stretch the dough toward the edges of the pan (ideally it will come within an inch or two) while pressing into it with your fingertips to create deep dimples, though not all the way to the bottom. Arrange the vegetables on the dough decoratively in a single layer, pressing them into the dough to help adhere. Brush with the remaining 1½ teaspoons olive oil, garnish with herbs and olives (if using), and sprinkle as much flaky salt as you like evenly over the surface.

Bake the flatbread until golden brown, puffed on the top, and crisp on the bottom, 28 to 40 minutes, rotating the pan halfway through. Place the pan on a wire rack to cool for 15 minutes. Carefully remove the bread from the pan, transfer to the rack, and let cool until just warm. Cut and serve.

SEELIE COURT CHEESE AND POTATO SOUP

MAKES ABOUT 2½ QUARTS

3 tablespoons unsalted butter

1 large yellow onion, chopped

1 large celery rib, trimmed and chopped

2 bay leaves

Kosher salt

1½ tablespoons pressed or grated garlic

2 teaspoons chopped fresh thyme

6 cups low-sodium chicken broth

1½ pounds russet potatoes, peeled and chopped

One 5.2-ounce package Boursin cheese flavored with garlic and fine herbs, crumbled and at room temperature, plus more cheese for garnish (optional)

¾ cup half-and-half

Freshly ground black pepper

¼ cup chopped fresh parsley

¼ cup snipped fresh chives

For those adventurers fortunate enough to dine shoulder to shoulder with the nature-loving Archfey of the Seelie Court, cheese and potato soup is a hearty, not-to-be-skipped starter that warms from the inside out. This slow-simmered, savory concoction is a delightful mix of potatoes, onions, celery, chives, and ripe herb-infused cream cheese. It is so delightful in fact that it has escaped the mystical confines of the Feywild, making its way within the bustling walls of the Sword Coast port metropolis of Baldur's Gate, to the iconic Elfsong Tavern, where it has become a regional favorite capitalizing on the cornucopia of fresh ingredients on offer. Regardless of where you sample this surprisingly light and tasty soup, the spirit of the Seelie Court original is in every spoonful.

In a large saucepan or medium pot over medium-high heat, melt the butter, swirling to coat the pan. Add the onion, celery, bay leaves, and 1 teaspoon salt and cook, stirring until the vegetables are heated through, about 3 minutes. Adjust the heat to medium-low, cover, and continue cooking, stirring occasionally, until the vegetables have released their juices, about 4 minutes. Add the garlic and thyme and cook, stirring, until fragrant, about 40 seconds. Add the chicken broth and potatoes, adjust the heat to medium-high, and bring to a boil. Adjust the heat to low, cover, and simmer until the potatoes are very tender, about 25 minutes. Remove and discard the bay leaves. Add the cheese, cover, and heat until the cheese softens or melts, about 2 minutes.

Remove the soup from the heat. Using an immersion blender, blend until smooth. Alternatively, let the soup cool slightly and blend in batches in a countertop blender. Return the soup to the saucepan, if necessary.

Adjust the heat to medium-low, add the half-and-half and 1 teaspoon salt, season with pepper, and warm the soup, stirring occasionally, until heated through, about 4 minutes. Add the parsley and about half the chives and stir to combine. Adjust the seasoning with additional salt and pepper, if necessary. Ladle into individual bowls and sprinkle with additional Boursin (if desired), and the remaining chives before serving.

ELFHARROW BAKED GOAT CHEESE

SERVES 6

3 ounces plain Melba toast

Kosher salt and freshly ground black pepper

½ cup minced shallots

1 egg

2 teaspoons Dijon mustard

One 10- to 12-ounce log firm, mild goat cheese, cut into 12 equal slices (see Cook's Note)

1 tablespoon red or white wine vinegar

2 teaspoons fresh lemon juice

¼ cup extra-virgin olive oil, plus more for brushing

12 cups loosely packed mixed salad greens or mesclun

1 apple or pear, cored and thinly sliced (optional)

3 tablespoons snipped fresh chives

COOK'S NOTES

To quickly and neatly slice the goat cheese, use a cheese slicer with a wire cutter. If you don't have one, you can use a length of dental floss, wrapping the ends around your index fingers so that it's taut.

If you prefer, you can use olive oil cooking spray to coat the frozen cheese rounds, rather than brushing them with olive oil.

Centuries of deforestation has caused the elves of Elfharrow to get more creative with their diets than those of their forest-based counterparts. Raising livestock has become a way of life for these elves, making dairy a central staple of their foodways. This traditional Elfharrow dish features medallions of goat cheese crusted in breadcrumbs and baked. The key ingredient, though, is a tangy mustard, said to originate in the Feywild, and the dish goes best with a green salad on the side. A word of caution: Don't try to source your ingredients in Elfharrow—these elves are quite a bit more territorial and protective than their northern cousins and a visit there could be your last.

In a food processor, combine the Melba toast and ½ teaspoon salt, season with pepper, and process until you have fine, uniform crumbs, about the texture of wheat germ. Add ¼ cup of the minced shallots and pulse to combine. Transfer the mixture to a shallow dish. In a second shallow dish, beat the egg and 1 teaspoon of the mustard until uniform. Dip a slice of goat cheese into the egg, covering both sides and the edges. Then dip into the Melba toast mixture, gently pressing the crumbs onto the cheese to form a thick coating, and place on a plate. Repeat with the remaining cheese slices, adding them to the plate as you go. Put the plate in the freezer and freeze until the cheese is very firm, about 45 minutes.

Meanwhile, in a large nonreactive bowl, combine the vinegar, lemon juice, remaining 1 teaspoon mustard, and ½ teaspoon salt; season with pepper; and whisk to incorporate. Stir in the remaining ¼ cup shallots and set aside for the flavors to blend, about 10 minutes. While whisking vigorously, add the olive oil in a slow, steady stream to blend and emulsify into a dressing. Adjust the seasoning with additional salt and pepper, if necessary, and set aside.

With a rack in the upper position, preheat the oven to 475°F. Set a wire rack in a rimmed baking sheet.

Place the frozen cheese rounds on the rack, then brush lightly all over with olive oil. Bake until the coating is deep golden brown and the cheese is slightly soft, 9 to 14 minutes. Let the cheese cool on the wire rack for about 2 minutes.

Whisk the dressing to recombine. Add the greens and apple (if using) to the dressing and toss to coat. Divide the greens among six serving plates, place two cheese rounds on each, and sprinkle with some of the chives. Serve immediately.

Harengon Coffee Carrots

SERVES 4

1½ pounds carrots, peeled and sliced on the diagonal ³⁄₈ inch thick

⅓ cup espresso or strong brewed coffee

1½ tablespoons molasses (not blackstrap)

Kosher salt

1½ tablespoons unsalted butter

1 teaspoon minced fresh thyme

¾ teaspoon balsamic vinegar

¼ teaspoon vanilla extract

Freshly ground black pepper

2 tablespoons chopped fresh parsley

Nothing says *harvest* like the colorful dish known as Harengon Coffee Carrots. An unexpected journey of flavors, fresh wild-picked carrots are simmered with mountain-grown kaeth (or coffee) and a generous amount of beet-derived molasses. A touch of thyme and finely aged balsamic vinegar round out this sweet and acidic treat, so perfectly balanced that even the eladrin of the Feywild often include it as a staple of their elaborate forest feasts. The harengon, rabbit-like denizens of the Feywild, famously prepare this dish with a veritable rainbow of orange, red, white, yellow, and purple carrots, emphasizing presentation as much as flavor. The inspired infusion of coffee provides a robust tang that will also add zip to anyone's step, especially the harengon who are known for their exuberance. When it comes to the serving table, this vibrant fall side is bound to bring you back for more.

In a medium nonstick skillet (with a lid) over medium-high heat, combine the carrots, espresso, molasses, and ¾ teaspoon salt and bring to a strong simmer. Cover, adjust the heat to medium, and let simmer, stirring occasionally, until the carrots feel almost tender when poked with the tip of a paring knife, 4 to 5 minutes. Add the butter and thyme, adjust the heat to high, and cook at a slow boil, uncovered, stirring to incorporate the butter as it melts, until the liquid is reduced to about 3 tablespoons and the carrots are tender and glazed, 4 to 5 minutes longer.

Remove the skillet from the heat, add the vinegar and vanilla, season with pepper, and stir to blend. Adjust the seasoning with additional salt and pepper, if necessary. Scrape the carrots and glaze into a serving dish and sprinkle with the parsley. Serve immediately.

BRACKLEBERRY JAM

MAKES ABOUT 1¼ CUPS

2 cups lightly packed, chopped fresh
strawberries (see Cook's Note)

½ cup fresh blueberries

½ cup fresh blackberries

½ cup plus 1 tablespoon granulated
sugar

1½ tablespoons fresh lemon juice

1 small pinch kosher salt

Brackleberry Jam is the Cormyrean moniker for a spread made from a medley of freshly foraged wild berries—one that has earned notoriety throughout the multiverse. While the Cormyr version utilizes strawberries, raspberries, blackberries, gooseberries, and even currants, all iterations of this well-traveled recipe call for fresh blueberries and sugar to properly flavor the mixture. A spritz of lemon and a dash of salt help to not only preserve the mash for canning but brighten the overall experience on the palate. Brackleberry Jam is as common as butter in the forest-heavy country of Cormyr, where its topography and climate yield an abundance of seasonal berries so plentiful they colorfully adorn the region's roads and trails. This jam spreads well on almost any warm loaf or muffin. In the Feywild, the berries are not only more bountiful but also more flavorful, resulting in an exquisite local variety of Brackleberry Jam.

Place a small plate in the freezer to chill.

In a medium saucepan over medium-high heat, combine the strawberries, blueberries, blackberries, sugar, lemon juice, and salt and bring to a strong boil, stirring to dissolve the sugar. Continue boiling for 5 minutes to soften the berries. Remove from the heat and, using a large slotted spoon or handheld potato masher, mash the berries thoroughly. Return to medium-high heat and continue to boil until the mixture is reduced and slightly thickened, just verging on a jammy consistency, 15 to 18 minutes longer.

Remove the plate from the freezer and drop about 1 teaspoon of the jam on it. Wait about 15 seconds and then run your finger through the jam. If it leaves a clean trail, the jam is done. If the jam runs back into the trail, return the plate to the freezer, turn the heat to medium, simmer the jam for 2 to 4 minutes longer before retesting. When the jam is done, transfer it to a heatproof jar and set aside to cool to room temperature (it will thicken as it cools). Cover with a tight-fitting lid and refrigerate for up to 3 weeks.

COOK'S NOTE

To chop the strawberries, hull them, cut each one in quarters lengthwise (large ones in sixths), turn the pieces 90 degrees, and cut them in half crosswise.

Fey Fritters

**MAKES ABOUT FOURTEEN
3-INCH FRITTERS**

4 cups water

Kosher salt

2 cups frozen (not thawed) or
fresh green peas

2 eggs, beaten

⅓ cup whole milk, plus more as needed

⅓ cup chopped fresh parsley

¼ cup minced shallot

1 teaspoon finely grated lemon zest

1 teaspoon baking powder

Freshly ground black pepper

½ cup all-purpose flour

½ cup coarsely crumbled feta

Neutral oil for panfrying

COOK'S NOTE

*If you like, accompany the fritters with
a small bowl of crème fraîche or a plain
Greek yogurt accented with a little olive
oil, lemon juice, chopped fresh mint or
scallions, salt, and pepper.*

No elven feast is complete without a basket (or three) of freshly fried sweet-pea Fey Fritters on offer. The nuanced yet indulgent combination of fresh sweet peas, shallots, and feta cheese is a match made in Arvandor, especially once handfuls of the bite-size bounty are dipped in batter and fried to perfection. From Prismeer to Evermeet, elves and those with whom they hold court relish these comforting table treats. Fey Fritters come with a warning: Once you try one, you'll want to spend all day eating these scrumptious snacks . . . and often, in the Feywild, you just do! It is believed that the recipe originated a millennium ago in the elven enclave of Evermeet, far before it was transported to the Plane of Faerie following the Spellplague. These tasty delicacies have been a mainstay on elven dining tables ever since.

Set a colander in the sink. Fill a large bowl with ice water and set aside. Line a plate with paper towels.

In a medium saucepan over high heat, bring the water to a rapid boil. Add ½ teaspoon salt and the peas, cover, and cook until bright green and just tender, about 2 minutes for frozen or 3 to 4 minutes for fresh (the water probably won't return to a full boil). Drain the peas in the colander and immediately place them in the ice water to stop the cooking. Drain the peas again and spread them on the prepared plate to dry. Set aside ⅓ cup.

Transfer the remaining peas to a food processor and pulse to a coarse puree, three or four 2-second pulses, then scrape the puree into a medium bowl. Add the reserved whole peas, eggs, milk, parsley, shallot, lemon zest, baking powder, and 1½ teaspoons salt; season with pepper; and stir to blend. Add the flour and, using a flexible spatula, fold it into the pea mixture. Add the feta and continue folding until no dry patches remain. This batter should be about the texture of a thick, chunky applesauce; if it's too thick, add more milk, 1 tablespoon at a time, folding to incorporate until the proper texture is attained.

With a rack in the middle position, preheat the oven to 250°F. Line a large plate or platter with paper towels and set aside.

In a large cast-iron or nonstick skillet over medium heat, warm 2 tablespoons neutral oil until shimmering. Gauge the oil temperature and seasoning by placing about 1 tablespoon batter in the center of the skillet and cook until the fritter is lightly browned on the bottom, about 1 minute (the oil around the fritters should bubble gently). Flip the fritter and cook until the second side is browned, about 1 minute longer. If it is too light or too dark, adjust the heat accordingly and retest. Taste and adjust the seasoning of the batter with additional salt and pepper, if necessary.

Working in batches, scoop roughly 3-tablespoon portions of the batter into the pan, spreading them into 3-inch rounds, with about 1 inch between them. Cook, undisturbed, until tiny bubbles appear on the surface and the bottom is browned, 2½ to 3 minutes. Using a spatula, gently flip the fritters and cook, undisturbed, until the second side is well browned, 1½ to 2 minutes longer. Transfer the fritters to the prepared plate and place in the oven to keep warm. Repeat to cook the remaining batter, adding more oil to equal about 2 tablespoons when necessary. Serve the fritters warm, as soon as the last batch has cooked.

Sprucebark Quaff

MAKES ABOUT 1½ QUARTS

4 large sprigs mint

½ large English cucumber, peeled and thinly sliced

6 cups cold water

COOK'S NOTES

Slapping the mint sprigs against your palm several times helps the leaves to release their flavor and fragrance.

Adding 1 or 2 thin slices of lemon imparts a subtle citrusy note.

A refreshing nonalcoholic aperitif, the drink known as Sprucebark Quaff is famous throughout the multiverse for not only preparing the palate for flavor but also freshening the breath after meals. A simple concoction of clean, fresh water; mint; and sweet cucumber, it is served at upscale taverns, inns, and temples across the Prime Material Plane but is especially popular in the Feywild and upper planes, where a similar mixture forms naturally in many ponds, lakes, and streams. It's believed to have been invented by Faerûnian elves as a method of purifying water, using plants to remove toxins. Whatever its origin, it is sure to recharge trail-weary adventurers no matter what planet or plane they roam.

In a large pitcher combine the mint, cucumber, and water. Refrigerate for 2 hours to infuse before serving.

ELDEEN BANQUET

SERVES 4

Kosher salt

2 pounds eggplant, peeled, stem ends trimmed, and cut lengthwise into ¾-inch-thick slices

½ cup all-purpose flour

Freshly ground black pepper

2 eggs

3½ cups panko breadcrumbs

1½ teaspoons crumbled dried oregano

1½ teaspoons paprika

1½ teaspoons garlic powder

1½ teaspoons onion powder

1 pinch cayenne pepper

½ cup olive oil (not extra-virgin)

SAUTÉED TOMATOES

1½ tablespoons extra-virgin olive oil

¼ cup minced shallot

Kosher salt

2 teaspoons pressed or grated garlic

3 cups cherry tomatoes or large grape tomatoes, halved

1 pinch granulated sugar

½ teaspoon sherry or balsamic vinegar

2 tablespoons chopped fresh parsley

2 tablespoons chopped fresh parsley

Despite its promise of a "banquet," the dish known as Eldeen Banquet is actually a hearty, one-dish meal sure to satisfy omnivores as much as vegetarians. Consisting of lightly breaded and fried eggplant topped with a warm, seasoned tomato sauce, this delight hails from the Eldeen Reaches, in the Khorvaire region of Eberron, which is noted for its robust forests and agriculture, and where the dish has occasionally migrated to the Feywild via a secret Fey Crossing. But while Eldeen Banquet is considered a regional delicacy, interpretations of the crispy, yet spongy, eggplant patty are common in esteemed eateries throughout the city of Sharn. High-end restaurants such as the Azure Gateway and the Celestial Vista, in the Skyway district, offer plates of Eldeen Banquet as delightful as their views. However, perhaps the best preparation is found in the unassuming Olladra's Arms, in the Hope's Peak district. Here, the portions are as generous as they are flavorful, ensuring the dish truly lives up to its moniker.

Line two baking sheets with clean kitchen towels or a triple layer of paper towels.

Sprinkle 1 tablespoon salt evenly over both sides of the eggplant slices to draw out its water and arrange the eggplant in a single layer on the prepared baking sheets. Allow to drain for about 1 hour, flipping the slices halfway through. Blot the eggplant dry with another clean kitchen towel or triple layer of paper towels, pressing firmly but taking care not to crush the eggplant. Transfer to a bowl or plate, and set aside. Wash and dry the baking sheets.

With racks in the upper- and lower-middle positions, place a baking sheet on each rack, and preheat the oven to 425°F. Line a large platter or third baking sheet with parchment paper and set aside.

In a shallow dish, such as a pie plate, combine the flour and 1 teaspoon pepper and whisk to incorporate. In a second shallow dish, beat the eggs until uniform. In a third shallow dish, combine the panko, oregano, paprika, garlic powder, onion powder, cayenne, ½ teaspoon salt, and 1 teaspoon pepper and stir to blend.

Working with one or two eggplant slices at a time, dredge them in the flour and tap off any excess. Dip the floured slices into the egg to coat thoroughly, allowing any excess to drip into the dish. Then dredge in the panko mixture to coat thoroughly, pressing the panko onto the eggplant to help adhere. Place the slices on the prepared platter, and repeat with the remaining eggplant slices, trying not to overlap them.

Carefully remove the preheated baking sheets from the oven. Add ¼ cup of the olive oil to each sheet and, using a heatproof silicone brush, spread it out evenly. Place half the breaded eggplant slices on each baking sheet in a single layer. Bake for 20 minutes and then flip the slices, rotating the baking sheets, and swap between the racks. Continue baking until the eggplant is well browned and crisp, 20 to 25 minutes longer.

To make the tomatoes: About 10 minutes after flipping the eggplant slices, in a medium skillet over medium heat, warm the olive oil. Add the shallot and ½ teaspoon salt and cook, stirring constantly, until the shallot starts to soften, about 2 minutes. Add the garlic and cook, stirring, until fragrant, about 40 seconds. Add the tomatoes, shake the pan to coat them with oil, and cook, shaking the skillet occasionally, until they soften but do not collapse completely, about 4 minutes, adding the sugar halfway through cooking. Add the vinegar and parsley and toss to distribute. Adjust the seasoning with additional salt if necessary.

Sprinkle the baked eggplant very lightly with salt. Transfer to a serving platter, spoon the tomatoes over or around the eggplant, and sprinkle with parsley. Serve immediately.

COOK'S NOTE

You'll need at least two, and preferably three, baking sheets. If you don't have a third, you can use a large cutting board for the dredged eggplant slices.

Saerloonian Glowfire

SERVES 2

2 sugar cubes, or 2 teaspoons granulated sugar

1 ounce ruby port

1 ounce Poire Williams eau-de-vie

6 ounces Prosecco or other sparkling wine, cold

2 thin slices fresh pear

It is said that *everything* in the Feywild is more beautiful—and more delicious. That is undoubtedly true when it comes to imbibing the already supernaturally delightful Saerloonian Glowfire. First concocted centuries ago in Saerloon, a Sembian metropolis known for its cultured and exotic tastes, Saerloonian Glowfire has become a notable export the Realms over. It has even made its way to Evermeet, an elven paradise transported to the Feywild long ago. While human in origin, this aromatic bracer, renowned equally for its alluring luminescence as for its refreshing hints of summer breezes and ripe pear, feels right at home filling the ornate wine flutes of high elven society.

Put a sugar cube in the bottoms of two champagne flutes. Pour ½ ounce port and ½ ounce Poire Williams into each flute and swirl to begin dissolving the sugar. Slowly add 3 ounces Prosecco to each one, and garnish with a slice of pear. Serve immediately.

Elverquisst

MAKES ABOUT 1¾ QUARTS

¼ cup granulated sugar

¼ cup warm water

One 750 ml bottle cold inexpensive, medium-bodied, dry red wine (such as Merlot)

1½ cups apple juice

1 cup pomegranate juice

½ cup Calvados or another brandy

3 cinnamon sticks

1 cup plain seltzer, cold

1 cup large ice cubes, plus more for serving

Apple slices for garnish (optional)

This autumnal aperitif of rare quality and divine taste is customarily served in conjunction with an elven high ceremony. Traditional Elverquisst vintages are distilled from orosks and resmers (rare summer fruits indigenous to Evereska) and sunshine, and it sips as smoothly as a cool mountain stream. Elves store their Elverquisst in crystal decanters capable of absorbing light and showcasing the tantalizing specks of gold dancing about in the rich claret mixture. According to legend, upon whispering a secret Elvish phrase, the sunlight streaming through the bottle will gather into thirteen points, resembling the constellation Correlian. Regardless, Elverquisst is highly prized by the elves and is a uniquely enchanting sip for curious imbibers who can get their hands on a bottle of this rare beverage.

In a large bowl or pitcher, combine the sugar and water and stir to dissolve the sugar. Add the wine, both juices, Calvados, and cinnamon sticks and stir. Cover and refrigerate for at least 4 hours or up to 24 hours.

When ready to serve, remove the cinnamon sticks, if desired. Add the seltzer and ice cubes and stir to blend. Pour into ice-filled punch or juice glasses, and garnish each with an apple slice, if desired.

Squirladax

FANGS! VamPEER or VamPIRE? Yeah, the second one. My mind screams, "Run Squirladax, into thine own traps!" With luck, a spike will gash my heart for I do not wish to rise a vampiric thrall. But I do not run. I will face this failure, this TPK.

Sasha

Skeletons charge up the slope and then EXPLOSIONS FROM THE HEAVENS! I look up to see. . . . No way! OUR SPELLJAMMER!?? WASN'T IT BROKEN!? And it's hurling fireballs at our enemies!!!

WAIT! Not fireballs. Those are flaming pieces of the spelljammer itself! OH CRAP! SHE'S COMING APART!

Bri'An

RINGING OF EAR, all is soot and dark fog. The Dashor has crashèd, sending all to scatter and yet striking **not one skeleton**! Vomited forth from the wreck is the dented, destroyèd, and motionless OTTER GNOME, DINT!

Squirladax breaks away to rush to Dint's side.

"Dint, my Arch-Nemesis. Dint, my oldest and truest friend!"

Didn't we kinda just meet Dint?

Sasha joins with tear-chokèd breaths. I look to my side and swear it be a single tear rolling from tiefling eye.

Squirladax's pleadings continue, "Brave Dint. I lost you once. I cannot bear to lose you again."

Then a slow-clap . . . and wicked chuckles from the darkest rain-soaked smog. Cresting the slope pasty Chahd and his smiling skeletons.

"Your hefty friend meets his end. And you're all food for fangs."

And to this, Dint croaked, "He lies."

Sasha and Dint locked eye to lens. She spoke simply.

"Then we shall press the truth from him."

Dint nodded.

AND SO DID SASHA HEAVE DINT ABOVE HER HEAD, AND BY TYR'S GRACE DID BOWL THE BALLLIKE BRONZE MAN DOWN THE HILL, SHATTERING MANY A'SHRIEKING SKELETONS!

The battle is joined!

Squirladax

The fog of war clears. All is bone and shatter. Nothing stands. Not even one friend.

But wait, hopeful reader! I see a cloistered group below! Huddled there is Deelia, cradling

a shivering man. I rush forth and my goblin eyes boggle with amazement. Deelia holds a crushèd and stabbèd Chahd! But to see the fear in his eyes, the blood on velveteen cape, and the broken **wooden fangs** hanging out his slackened jaw, he can only simply be "Chad."

Chad chokes out, "You were right, Deelia. Neither I vampire nor vampeer. It's just . . . I started hanging out with skeletons after Shadow's Edge burned down, and you know, they're super judgy. I just wanted them to like me."

Deelia sobs, "Then 'twas I that did this, Chad. Destroyed our school with flame, I did, and your only crime was to run screaming while ablaze to the Lords! . . . A tattle move, but still!"

See us all, Deelia's vexing was always of her own making, and thus did she comfort Chad by casting away the rain's chill . . . **with a gentle flame from her snapping fingers**, her powers restorèd by mercy.

Chad's shivering abated, his eyes glazed as death approached. Would not Deelia be pleasèd, as Chad's soul could now be whispered to her Raven Queen? But even as Chad's body went limp, she whispered through tears—

"Please . . ."

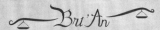

Bri'An

SO IT WAS THAT TYR'S SERVANT BRI'AN SNAPPÈD FORTH LIMBS AND SHINS AND CHINNY CHIN CHINS OF THE DAMNED IN HIS BATTLE 'GAINST UNDEATH. NOBLY HE FOUGHT, KILLING THE DEAD UNTO A DOUBLE-DEATH WHENCE NO SKELETON, SHALL 'ERE RETURN TO SNEER UPON THE LIVING.

And as Bri'An could deliver death to the dead, so might he deliver life unto the living? Thusly, the scoundrel dragonborn—himself for the first time in his life—did layeth hands on the frail Chad. And Tyr's grace fell as a rain, melting away eyeshadows and other gothic makeups off the visage of Chad, who was deliverèd unto Tyr's Grace, ALIVE! So Sayeth We Thusly.

Praise be to being one's self.

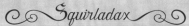

Squirladax

Persistent reader, how we feasted in victory that day. Famished, we returnèd to the inn, where our newly re-pioused Bri'An has shared Tyr's favor with us all! He has summoned a HEROES' FEAST of elven flatbreads, harengon coffee carrots, and the freshest of sprucebark quaff for all to sup!

'Twas at that moment that mangled Dint lurched in the doorway, held up by Sasha and Deelia, his gut-gears still churning by the grace of his Otter Gnome gods.

A tear running down my face, I placed a hand upon the pauldroned shoulder of my shadowy double and spoketh thus: "You can keep your Astral Diamonds, dear Master of Treason."

AFTERWORD: PLAYING WITH YOUR FOOD

Every group that sits down around a table to play *Dungeons & Dragons* can find its own style, its own groove. You may play epic sessions that start in the afternoon and run until the wee hours of the night. Or you may do lots of short, intensive episodes. Your adventures may be all about intrigue, or white-knuckle combat, or just light silly fun—or they may explore the deep lore of the multiverse, searching for an ever-deeper understanding of the fantastic worlds that D&D opens up to us all.

The adventures of the Bureau of Dark Tables are mostly wacky hijinks, but they also revolve around food. That doesn't mean anyone else's stories have to do the same, but every group's adventure in D&D should follow their bliss. One of the great joys of traveling in real life is to experience the cuisines of different cultures first-hand—we live in a world where many things from distant lands can be shipped conveniently to our doorstep, but freshly prepared food, done in the style of its place of origin, is something you must travel to experience. The Bureau of Dark Tables are the sort of adventurers who know that, wherever your triumphs and perils take you, you haven't really been there unless you've taken in the local fare. Whatever your ostensible main quest may be, your side quest is always to level up your palate.

In this book, there are recipes that can help you as a player to deepen your bond with both your characters and your gaming group. If you and your friends want to take your connection to the D&D multiverse into the culinary space, these recipes can become part of your game experience as well as your mealtimes. A refreshing Ray of Frost or a slice of Laumberry Pie can be as much of a reward as the experience points you get after an epic adventure.

But as with any undertaking, getting the best results requires planning ahead. Inserting the whole process of making and eating a meal into a game session can be a challenge unto itself. So bear in mind you will need:

Rule #1: Support. Every great band of adventurers plays to everyone's strengths. If you are the Dungeon Master (DM), it might be best to leave the cooking to someone else. You are already doing all of the preparatory work for the adventure. Many DMs offer up their homes for play, and if you are hosting, you may feel responsible for keeping everyone else fed. So players, show your thanks to the DM by volunteering to bring the food!

If your group plays at your local friendly game store, or some other public space that likely does not have a full kitchen, you should plan ahead. You might find a fridge and a microwave there that can hold a few Tupperware containers, if you are lucky. Some dishes you can prepare ahead of time that will transport well to a game include the Halfling Iron Rations or Fig Cakes. If you know you have an oven for heating up food when you get there, then you might consider bringing Ornabra or Sensate Palate Cleanser.

Don't forget that cooking, and eating, can make a mess, but not all dishes are equally messy. Some recipes, such as Tamarind Balls, Goldenstars, and Cloaks, don't require players to have their own plates and utensils. But wherever you are bringing the food, have a plan for how to deal with any leftovers, and how not to leave a dish disaster in your wake.

One fun way to use this cookbook is to try to match the food your group eats with the adventure you are playing. Whatever city of the D&D multiverse your party is visiting, or whichever wilderness you camp in, there are dishes that can put you in your character's shoes. You may not have the appetite to sample everything that the Bureau of Dark Tables eats as they make their way around Realmspace, but you can still make meals the centerpiece of your adventure.

Rule #2: Plan. Don't have a Total Planning Katastrophe. Schedule serious meals for the beginning or end of a play session. If you are doing a real marathon and you need to have a full meal in the middle, take a break from the game. Some of the dishes in this cookbook, like Tavern Crickets and Black Lotus Root, make for good snacks around the table, but if you're laying out a multi-course cornucopia, you're going to need the table space. As a rule of thumb, if you need to have utensils and plates out to eat, then set the dice and character sheets away until you're done. You don't want to have to fish a d4 out of your Two Hares Inn Rabbit Stew.

There's nothing better than taking an hour after a D&D session to decompress with your friends over a refreshing dinner, chatting about the ups and downs of the day. These post-game sessions can actually make a big difference in your campaigns—it helps everyone to get on the same page about game events, and it may even lead to some inspirations for the next session. And if your session runs all night, there are some great breakfast options in this book, like the Green Onion Pancakes.

There are a few ways to integrate eating into the play of D&D. If you know in advance that the party is going to attend a banquet in Ravenloft, you can always arrange to have the meal ready for the players to enjoy in real-time as they role play their characters. This requires some coordination, but it can really bring the game world to life, with a little mood lighting, music, and maybe even costumes.

But if you're going to build a meal into your D&D session, you probably aren't going to be able to make it from scratch during a quick break. Choose dishes where most of the preparatory work can be done before the session starts, where it will only take a few minutes to heat things up and get them on the table. Duergar Smoked Herring and Boar Hock Soup are examples of good choices where you can do a lot of the work beforehand and then heat them up at the last minute. You definitely want to avoid trying to make something like Fire-Wrapped Golden Fish while you are in the middle of a play session, because if you get distracted and leave it cooking for too long, it could easily burn and the smell of this rare aquatic treat will no doubt linger until next week's session.

Rule #3: Improvise. Every DM knows that sometimes you just have to wing it—rules are guidelines, and to keep up the flow of play you may have to do what seems right rather than leafing through rulebooks. Every chef knows the same rule: You have to work with what you've got, and sometimes that means taking a different path than the printed recipe.

Most importantly, these recipes are intended to inspire your creativity. It would be impossible to cram the flavors of the multiverse into this cookbook, or a whole series of them—so take the recipes here as examples. Once you have a sense for the palates of the planes, you can use those as building blocks for developing your own recipes in the spirit of these guidelines.

Once you get the hang of it, you can develop your own recipes. And if you are having trouble deciding between ingredients, remember that you are a D&D player: you can always roll for it! For example, you could assign tofu, chicken, pork, and beef each to a number on a d4. Give it a roll, and whatever number lands becomes the accompanying protein for that tasty Chopforest. But like any good DM, if the result of the die roll doesn't feel right, don't be afraid to exercise a little "divine intervention" and reroll. Sometimes it takes a die roll to tell you what your real preference would be.

Dine on!

ACKNOWLEDGMENTS

In order to bring this project together, it certainly took a village. This work would not have been possible without the help, support, and dedication of countless individuals outside of the author team. Firstly, we would like to thank every D&D designer, artist,

and staff member who contributed to this incredible game over the last nearly fifty years. Your work and contributions continue to be an inspiration to us and to the millions of D&D fans across the globe—thank you! Next, our infinite love and thanks to our families and friends—while too many to count, they are our constant source of love, support, and inspiration. Then, to the people and organizations that truly made this piece possible: thank you to the incredible efforts and talents of Aaron Wehner (publisher and the original idea!), Shaida Boroumand (project editor), Claire Yee (project editor), Doug Ogan (production editor), Kelly Booth (art director), Emma Campion (photo director), Mari Gill (production designer), Dan Myers (production manager), Jane Chinn (prepress color manager), Deborah Kops (copyeditor), Lauren Ealy (publicist), and the rest of the amazing team at Ten Speed Press, who shared our passion and vision for this project. Thank you also to those who helped us bring this project to life including master chef Adam Ried, photographer Ray Kachatorian, food stylist Nicole Twohy, prop master Glenn Jenkins, and the talented artists at Conceptopolis. Our sincerest thanks and appreciation to the team at D&D publisher Wizards of the Coast, who not only allowed this project to take place but helped us in countless ways. Special thanks to Paul Morrissey, Nathan Stewart, Liz Schuh, Hilary Ross, and all the other fine folks who played a part "on screen" or behind the scenes. A hearty thank-you to our literary agent, Jacques de Spoelberch, who flawlessly managed the business side of things and offered us continuous support and guidance. Last, but not least, thank you to the fans who are the true ingredients of D&D.

ABOUT THE AUTHORS

KYLE NEWMAN is an author and award-winning filmmaker who has directed numerous feature films including the *Star Wars*–fueled comedy *Fanboys*; *Barely Lethal*, starring Samuel L. Jackson for A24 Films; Lionsgate / Prime Video's esports comedy *1UP* and co-directed the *Dungeons & Dragons 50th Anniversary Documentary* for Hasbro, Inc. He has directed the music industry's top artists including Taylor Swift, Lana Del Rey, and Katy Perry, and produced the acclaimed documentaries *Raiders!: The Story of the Greatest Fan Film Ever Made* and *A Disturbance in the Force*. As an author, he is known for his work on *Dungeons & Dragons: Art & Arcana*, the *New York Times* bestseller *Heroes' Feast: The Official D&D Cookbook*, and *Dungeons & Dragons: Lore & Legends*. Newman, an honors graduate of NYU's Tisch School of Film/Television and a member of the Directors Guild of America, resides in Los Angeles with his partner Cyn and their children.

JON PETERSON is widely recognized as an authority on the history of games, best known as the author of *Playing at the World* (2012), *The Elusive Shift* (2020), and *Game Wizards* (2021). He also co-authored *Dungeons & Dragons: Art & Arcana* (2018) and *Heroes' Feast: The Official D&D Cookbook* (2020). He has contributed to academic anthologies on games, including MIT Press's *Zones of Control* (2016) and Routledge's *Role-Playing Game Studies: Transmedia Foundations* (2018). Jon also has written for various geek culture websites, including Wired, Polygon, and BoingBoing, as well as maintaining his own blog.

MICHAEL WITWER is a *New York Times*–bestselling author known for his work on the Hugo-nominated *Dungeons & Dragons: Art & Arcana*, the critically acclaimed *Empire of Imagination: Gary Gygax and the Birth of Dungeons & Dragons*, and the bestselling *Heroes' Feast: The Official D&D Cookbook*. His most recent works include *Dungeons & Dragons: The Legend of Drizzt Visual Dictionary* (DK 2023), *Dungeons & Dragons: Lore & Legends* (Penguin Random House 2023), and his debut novel, *Vivian Van Tassel and the Secret of Midnight Lake* (Simon & Schuster 2023). He holds degrees from Northwestern University and the University of Chicago and resides in Chicago, Illinois, with his wife, two daughters, and two sons.

SAM WITWER is an actor and musician with a love of the fantasy and science fiction genres. He is best-known for a series of sci-fi genre roles spanning a twenty-year career. He led SyFy's darkly humorous and provocative drama series, *Being Human*, playing vampire-gone-straight Aidan Waite (8+3 Hit Dice). Other credits include Raptor Pilot Crashdown in the Hugo Award–winning series *Battlestar Galactica*, Superman-killing Doomsday in CW's *Smallville*, Mr. Hyde in ABC's *Once Upon a Time*, and supporting roles in Showtime's *Dexter*, Amazon's *Electric Dreams*, and Stephen King and Frank Darabont's cult-classic horror film, *The Mist*. Sam is also well-known for his continuing work for the Star Wars saga, bringing various characters to life in video games, film, and television, starting in 2008 as Starkiller in *Star Wars: The Force Unleashed*, and culminating, most recently, in a multi-year, Emmy-nominated run voicing the ex-Sith lord Darth Maul. Recently, Sam played Agent Liberty on WB's *Supergirl* and served as the main character in Sony's bestselling *Days Gone* video game. He is a longtime and avid player of both electronic games and pen-and-paper role-playing games, and he hosts a regular Twitch broadcast where his gaming chops are on display.

INDEX

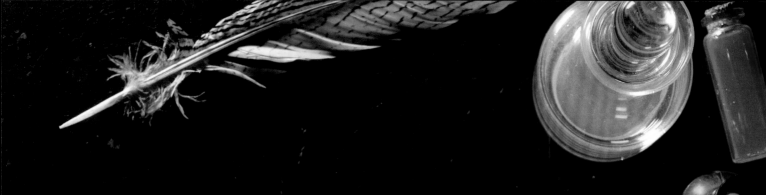

Published in the United States by Ten Speed Press, an imprint of the Crown Publishing Group, a division of Penguin Random House LLC, New York. TenSpeed.com

Ten Speed Press and the Ten Speed Press colophon are registered trademarks of Penguin Random House LLC.

Typefaces: Jim Parkinson's Tiamat, Edward Benguiat's ITC Barcelona, P22 Type Foundry's P22 Declaration Pro, and Ahmet Altun's Harman

Library of Congress Cataloging-in-Publication Data is on file with the publisher.

Hardcover ISBN: 978-1-9848-6131-3
eBook ISBN: 978-1-9848-6132-0
B&N Special Edition ISBN: 978-1-9848-6326-3

Printed in China

Publisher: Aaron Wehner
Project editors: Shaida Boroumand and Claire Yee
Production editors: Doug Ogan and Natalie Blachere
Art director and designer: Kelly Booth
Photo director: Emma Campion
Production designers : Mari Gill and Faith Hague
Production manager: Dan Myers
Prepress color manager: Jane Chinn
Photo retoucher: Tamara White
Photo assistant: Jeff Johnson
Location: Castello di Amorosa Winery
Food stylist: Nicole Twohy | Food stylist assistants: Genesis Vallejo and Allison Fellion
Prop stylist: Glenn Jenkins | Prop stylist assistants: Zach Wine and Cindy Chesney
Copyeditor: Deborah Kops | Proofreader: Linda Bouchard | Indexer: Ken DellaPenta
Publicist: Lauren Ealy | Marketer: Ashleigh Heaton
Wizards of the Coast team: Paul Morrissey
Illustrators: Conceptopolis, LLC | Character portrait illustrator: Simon Taylor | Decorative art designers: Marisa Kwek and Kelly Booth

10 9 8 7 6 5 4 3 2 1

First Edition

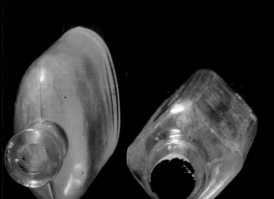